THEOLOGICAL NOTEBOOK II

Date Due			
		DISCARDED	

Theological Notebook

VOLUME II ~ 1964 — 1968

DONALD G. BLOESCH

HELMERS & HOWARD

COLORADO SPRINGS

Published by Helmers & Howard, Publishers, Inc.
P.O. Box 7407, Colorado Springs, CO 80933 USA.

LIBRARY OF CONGRESS CATALOGING-IN-PUBLICATION DATA
(Revised for volume 2)

Bloesch, Donald G., 1928-
  Theological notebook.

  (The spiritual journals of Donald G. Bloesch ;
1st-   )
  Includes bibliographical references and indexes.
  Contents: v. 1. 1960-1964 — v. 2. 1964-1968.
  1. Meditations. 2. Theology. I. Title. II. Series: Bloesch, Donald G.,
1928-   . Spiritual journals of Donald G. Bloesch ; 1st, etc.
BV4832.2.B545 1st   230'.44 s   [230'.044]   88-24566
ISBN 0-939443-12-0 (v. 1)
ISBN 0-939443-13-9 (v. 2)

Printed in the United States of America

CONTENTS

Preface vii

About the Author. ix

1964. 1

1965. 21

1966. 74

1967 123

1968 142

Bibliography: The Published Writings

of Donald G. Bloesch, 1952 — 1991. 181

Index of Subjects. 198

Index of Names 212

Index of Scriptures .214

To
my cousin,
Daniel Bloesch

PREFACE

WHILE STANDING BY most of my affirmations in this second volume of my *Theological Notebook*, as might be expected, I no longer subscribe to everything said there. I am now much more reluctant to include self-love in agape. I do believe, however, that agape love makes a place for legitimate self-concern and self-respect. I would also portray Christ's sacrifice as not simply an offer of salvation but as the enactment of salvation, though always in correlation with the decision of faith. Again, I now hold that infants, even unborn children, are persons, not just individuals, because they are already in a personal relationship with God. Scripture makes it clear that from our birth, and even before, we are sought out and addressed by God (cf. Pss. 22:9-10, 71:6, 139:13-16; Isa. 49:1, 5; Jer. 1:5; Luke 1:41-44). Finally, speculation concerning the eternal destiny of infants, whether or not they are included in the wider covenant family, I now consider unwise.

Although there are places where I have substituted inclusive people language, I have, for the most part, continued to leave my language intact, since this was the mode of expression at that time.

I wish to thank both my wife Brenda and Kathy Yanni of

Helmers and Howard Publishing Company for their diligent copyediting and proofreading of this manuscript.

August 1991

ABOUT THE AUTHOR

DONALD G. BLOESCH is professor of systematic theology at the University of Dubuque Theological Seminary in Dubuque, Iowa. His educational background includes the B.A. degree from Elmhurst College in Illinois, the B.D. from Chicago Theological Seminary, the Ph.D. in theology from the University of Chicago, postdoctoral study at the Universities of Oxford, Basel, and Tübingen, and an honorary doctor of divinity degree from Doane College. He has studied under such noted theologians as Karl Barth, Hans Küng, and Leonard Hodgson abroad; and under Charles Hartshorne, Daniel Jenkins, Wilhelm Pauck, Jaroslav Pelikan, and Daniel Day Williams at the University of Chicago. His mentors include his colleague Arthur C. Cochrane, professor emeritus at Dubuque Theological Seminary.

Dr. Bloesch, who has pastored congregations as an ordained minister in the United Church of Christ, comes from a family of pastors and missionaries. His two grandfathers, both of whom studied at evangelical mission schools in Switzerland (St. Chrischona and the Basel Mission), came to the United States as missionaries to German-speaking immigrants. Donald Bloesch's father was an ordained minister in the Evangelical Synod of North America (now UCC), and as a young man used to drive Reinhold Niebuhr around in a horse and buggy when Niebuhr was trying to earn money selling books. The Niebuhrs and Bloeschs were family friends; Donald Bloesch would later write his dissertation on Reinhold Niebuhr's apologetics.

A prolific writer of books, articles, and reviews, Dr. Bloesch has dedicated much of his life work to maintaining an evangelical witness in pluralistic environments. He lectures at seminaries, colleges, and church conferences in addition to teaching at Dubuque. He is past president of the American Theological Society (Midwest Div.) and is advisor to renewal groups within mainline denominations. Dr. Bloesch's wife, Brenda, who received the Ph.D. in French literature from the University of London, assists him in his work by serving as his research associate and as copyeditor of all his writings.

1964

OCTOBER 15 — DECEMBER 14

~ Salvation ~

Against orthodox Calvinism I maintain that we are saved not only *through* faith but also *by* faith. This is to say, we are not only passive recipients of the grace of God but also active participants in this grace. Faith involves not only God's gift but our decision as well. Nevertheless, our decision is made possible by God's Spirit; our cooperation with God is grounded not in our free will but solely in free grace.

The author of our salvation is the holy God, but the medium of our salvation is the holy humanity of Jesus.

~ Fear ~

There is a difference between a healthy fear of God and a neurotic or morbid fear of hell. Jesus tells us to fear him who is able to cast us into hell (Luke 12:4-5), but we are not told to direct our fear toward hell as such.

1

~ Revelation ~

Revelation can be defined as the conjunction of the moment of incarnation and the moment of existential decision.

The true theologian will seek to stand only on the solid rock of revelation, not on the quicksand of natural reason.

~ Faith ~

The experience of faith is not accessible to psychological study, although its outward effects can be subjected to scientific scrutiny.

Faith is not a matured possession of victory but a striving toward victory.

Faith is an intangible reality, psychic in nature, imperceptible to the senses, and incomprehensible to reason (Adolf Köberle).

The decision of faith both confirms and fulfills the sacrament of baptism. This decision signifies not a new baptism of the Spirit but the fruit and flower of this baptism.

Faith can bring us to the holy city, but only free grace can open the gate.

~ *The Victorious Life* ~

The victorious life is a struggle toward victory rather than an accomplished victory.

~ *Saints* ~

The giants in the faith have been weak men and women who depended fully upon God in the fulfillment of their tasks.

It has been said that all people have their price, but certainly the saints are exceptions.

~ *Mysticism* ~

In Barth's theology the subject-object relation is maintained in the experience of faith, but this relation is now transfigured. In Tillich's theology the subject-object relation is entirely transcended.

~ *My Vocation* ~

I conceive my area of specialization at this seminary to be the encounter of the Christian faith with the modern secular world and the kind of witness (both in word and deed) that such an encounter entails. My basic concern is the renewal and reformation of the church in a secular society.

I often pray to God: "Make me a saint before a scholar; grant me piety before academic proficiency."

My goals in life can be placed in this order: a person of prayer; a servant of the Word, who preaches with power and authority; a loving husband; a dedicated teacher; and a proficient writer.

~ God ~

God is not only the ground of being but also the highest being. He is to be found not only in the depths but also in the heights.

~ Incorporation into the Church ~

Barth holds that we are incorporated into the church through the crucifixion and resurrection of Christ. Roman Catholic and Lutheran theologians believe that we are incorporated into the church through baptism. Calvin's position, which I think is more sound than the others, is that we are united with the church through baptism *and* faith.

~ Religious Liberty ~

The theological basis of religious liberty is not the common good nor the dignity of the individual, but God's act for humankind in Jesus Christ which calls for a *free* decision.

~ The Historical Jesus ~

I affirm not the "historical Jesus," the Jesus who is accessible to historical investigation and verification, but the historic Jesus Christ, the Jesus who is known in the community of faith as the crucified and reigning Lord by virtue of his resurrection from the dead.

~ *Miracles* ~

Oswald T. Allis, formerly a member of the Old Testament department at Princeton Theological Seminary, gives this definition of a miracle: "In the narrowest biblical sense, miracles are events in the external world, wrought by the immediate power of God and intended as a sign or attestation" (*Christianity Today*, 6 Nov. 1964). My objection to this definition is that it makes a miracle accessible to the senses and thus loses sight of the hidden and mysterious character of an act of God. It also limits miracles to the intervention of God in nature and does not consider the marvelous workings of God in and through natural processes.

~ *The Christian Life* ~

A Christian life contributes to our salvation because it strengthens faith, not because it accumulates merit.

Saints give themselves to all, but they belong only to God.

~ *Progressive Sanctification* ~

I hold to the progressive sanctification of Christians (Calvin), but not to their entire sanctification in this life (Wesley).

My theology upholds both entire sanctification and progressive sanctification. Entire sanctification is our standard and goal; progressive sanctification is the means by which we proceed toward this goal.

The most authentic kind of prayer is humble supplication, casting ourselves upon the mercy and love of our Heavenly Father. This is one of the highest forms of prayer because it reveals our absolute dependence upon God.

Meditation on a spiritual theme is not prayer in the proper sense, but it can place us in the presence of God and open the door to communion with God.

~ Regeneration ~

God grants us regeneration immediately in the act of repentance, but he does not grant it all at one time. Regeneration is not fully ours until we have discarded this earthly body and entered into the realm of the spirit.

~ Salvation ~

Roman Catholicism holds that our salvation can be gained or earned. Barthianism contends that our salvation can only be acknowledged and proclaimed. I affirm that our salvation cannot be earned but must be appropriated and realized in a Christian life.

~ Revivalism ~

My objections to evangelical revivalism are fourfold: (1) it speaks of regeneration as being given all at one time in the act of decision; (2) it places the locus of salvation in a specific conversion experience; (3) it underplays the role of the sacraments in our salvation; (4) it does not perceive the Lordship of Christ over the entire world, which perhaps accounts for its devaluation of social and political action.

~ Religious Communities ~

The three perils that confront a religious community are ghettoism, pharisaism, and archaism. The new Protestant communities are perhaps in most danger of the last.

~ Relativism ~

In the age of rationalism, mortals sought to be little gods. In the present period of relativism, we find neither gods nor mortals but the ghosts of mortals.

~ Fallen-away Christians ~

Luther held that Christians who have fallen must return to their baptism. Spener said that they stand in need of a new regeneration. I believe they must resume the struggle toward full regeneration through daily repentance and obedience.

~ Prayer ~

Prayer proceeds on the basis of pure faith, not on the basis of a felt presence of God (although this may occur). Prayer is a venture of faith, not a quest for signs or miracles. Prayer is not basking in the light of God but walking with God in the darkness, sometimes even striving with God in the darkness.

Prayer relates to the mystical dimension of faith. In prayer we are grasped by the Spiritual Presence and lifted above ourselves, often oblivious to what is happening to us.

7

~ Despair and Faith ~

According to William Stringfellow it is not despair that is the precondition of the gospel but instead a radical exposure to the harsh realities of the human situation. We must face up to our lostness and to the terrible reality of death before we can turn to God. My question is: Can we be confronted with our lostness apart from an overwhelming experience of the love of Jesus Christ on Calvary?

~ Equality in Sin ~

Human beings are equal in their unworthiness before God, but they are not equal in their bondage to sin.

~ Dependence on God ~

Dependence on other people is servile dependence; dependence on God is liberating dependence.

~ Marriage ~

Only a Christian marriage is a remedy for sin in the full sense, since Christ, who alone overcomes sin, is present in such a marriage.

~ Timidity ~

On his deathbed Calvin acknowledged that he was by nature timid and fearful. I must certainly make the same confession. My hope is that my timidity and fear might on occasion be transmuted into a holy boldness and confidence through God's Spirit.

~ Divine Solace ~

We are often tempted to seek our strength and comfort in our loved ones rather than in God. Our loved ones can give us much solace, but they cannot give us the inward peace that comes only from God.

~ Wisdom ~

In and of myself I am woefully ignorant. If I happen at times to speak words of wisdom, the credit belongs to the Holy Spirit, who dwells within all Christians.

~ Asceticism ~

There is an asceticism of sexual love, which simply means the disciplining and channeling of these passions in the direction of conjugal union.

The Bible teaches an asceticism not only of the body but also of the spirit. This is the primary asceticism in that the spirit is the seat of sin.

~ The Solitary Life ~

A solitary life to the glory of God is a good thing, but this must not be confused with an isolated life, a life that disengages us from the needs and sorrows of others.

9

~ *Radicalism* ~

We need radicalism in the sense of going deep, but we must eschew the radicalism that means going far out.

1964

DECEMBER 15 — DECEMBER 31

~ *Struggle* ~

The pagan is engaged in a struggle to exist. The Christian is engaged in a struggle to conquer.

~ *Membership in the Kingdom* ~

The whole world is *under* Christ's kingship, but only those who are united with Christ in faith are *in* his kingdom.

All people are *under* the kingdom of light, but only those who have faith are *in* the kingdom of light.

~ *Faith and Love* ~

Faith is accompanied and strengthened by love, but not completed by love. Love is the fruit and goal of faith, but not the form or perfection of faith.

In contemporary theology, love is often spoken of as the prime fruit of faith. But is not a clearer understanding of the truth also a fruit of faith? Can faith and love be separated from truth?

~ *The Suffering of Faith* ~

The suffering of faith takes the form of either suffering vicariously for others or suffering persecution.

Because of their faith Christians will experience four types of suffering: vicarious suffering for others; persecution and rejection; the pain of remembering Christ's passion; and the suffering of repentance.

We will suffer either ignominiously for our sins or heroically for the faith.

We will suffer either the pangs of guilt and despair or the anguish of vicarious love.

~ *Prayer Groups* ~

Any church that has prayer groups should also have discussion groups on social problems. Prayer must always be integrally related to life in the world.

~ *Conversion* ~

I recently heard a noted evangelical preacher maintain that the basis for a fully Christian social order lies in the conversion of individuals as opposed to social reforms. But this assumption would hold true only if conversion predicated perfection.

~ *Marriage* ~

Just as the only kind of marriage that can be said to be ordained by God is a marriage "in the Lord," so the only kind of state that can be regarded as being expressly sanctioned by God is a just state.

Roman Catholic theology sees marriage as purified and transfigured by grace, but it does not see marriage as reconstituted and relativized by grace. For Roman Catholic theology the fundamental purpose of marriage remains the same — procreation and fertility. For radical evangelical Protestantism the purpose of marriage itself is changed. The purpose of a marriage in the Lord can be none other than kingdom service.

The Roman Catholic doctrine of marriage is marred by its double standard regarding Christian service (*diakonia*). Those who are called to full-time Christian service must place themselves under the "counsels of perfection" — celibacy, poverty, and obedience. Christians who earn their way in the world are regarded as part-time servants of Christ, and thereby the vocational character of marriage is obscured.

The sexual act in Christian marriage must be seen not as a means to an end but rather as an end within a more comprehensive end — partnership in service.

Modern culture makes too much of marriage and at the same time too little. We regard marriage as the key to self-fulfillment, whereas only Christ can be the fulfillment of our lives. At the same time, we see marriage as a biological and social necessity and thereby lose sight of marriage as a vocation to kingdom service, which is certainly what Paul means when he speaks of marriage "in the Lord."

In Catholic theology marriage is purified and perfected by grace, but it still rests on a natural foundation. In the theology associated with the Radical Reformation marriage itself is placed on a new foundation — the gospel of free grace and the service of Jesus Christ.

The deepest tie connecting the two partners in a Christian marriage is spiritual. This is why they will regard themselves first of all as brother and sister in Christ and secondarily as husband and wife. The spiritual relation is eternal, whereas the biological relation is temporal.

In Catholic theology celibate priests and members of monastic orders are believed to be the ones called to "religious" work. Ordinary Christians are called to "secular" work. The concern of the former is the worship of God and the extension of the church in the world. The primary concern of the latter is home and family, although ordinary Christians must also serve the mission of the church, but indirectly — by supporting the priestly ministry and the monastic orders. But is not the foremost purpose of marriage and family also the building of the kingdom? Should not a married couple also be full-time servants of the kingdom?

14

~ Divorce ~

Divorce between two partners in the covenant of marriage is always a manifestation of sin and personal failure, but this does not mean that both partners are equally guilty. Divorce may be a commandment of God once the spiritual ties are broken, even by only one of the partners.

~ Nature and Grace ~

Modern paganism enthrones the natural. Protestant liberalism accepts the natural. Roman Catholicism wishes to purify and change the natural. Evangelical theology seeks to redirect and renew the natural.

Roman Catholicism emphasizes the purification and transcendence of the natural. Liberal Protestantism encourages the acceptance of the natural. Biblical faith places the accent on the conversion and rechanneling of the natural.

Both Roman Catholic and Evangelical theologies advocate the conversion of the natural, but in different senses. Roman Catholicism seeks the purification and transcendence of the natural. Evangelical theology seeks the restoration and renewal of the natural.

In Roman Catholic theology, grace perfects and transfigures nature and thereby lifts nature above itself. In Evangelical theology, grace converts and renews nature and thereby points nature in a new direction.

In Roman Catholic theology, the contrast is between grace and nature. In Evangelical theology, the contrast is between grace and sin.

~ Bearing the Cross ~

The cross that Christ places upon us is not a burden but a shield, which enables us to vanquish the powers of darkness.

~ The New Birth ~

When one becomes a Christian, one is not only turned in a new direction but also given a new nature.

~ Faith ~

Since God's revelation is both word and deed, faith must be both an assent of the mind and an act of the will.

~ Doubt ~

Questioning doubt is a sign of common grace; despairing doubt is the final fruit of original sin.

~ Salvation ~

Calvin spoke of the necessity for baptism and personal decision as well as the reality of predestination. He also held to the idea of the covenant community whereby the children of believers are born into the domain of grace. Theologians today also need to speak of these things.

~ *Authority* ~

The criterion in my theology is not simply God speaking in the Scriptures but God speaking to our hearts through his Spirit. Word and Spirit must forever be united if we are to escape the perils of biblicism on the one hand and spiritualism on the other.

~ *Sacred and Secular* ~

The Christian faith affirms not that everything in the world is holy but that anything might become holy under the impact of the Spirit.

Life in the world as such is not sacramental, but particular activities in the world may become sacramental when the Holy Spirit is acting in and through these activities for our salvation.

There are certain activities that can be regarded as "religious" as opposed to "secular" in that they are indissolubly related to the redemptive action of the Spirit of Christ. Among these are prayer, Bible reading, the hearing of the Word, and witnessing. But any secular activity may also become a means of grace on certain occasions, viz. when the Spirit is acting for our salvation.

The sacred and the secular will be united in a creative synthesis only in the kingdom of God, which is still to come. According to the book of Revelation, in the new Jerusalem there will be no need of a temple.

17

~ Witnessing and Service ~

Witness without service is empty; service without witness is dumb (Alan Walker).

~ Mysticism ~

I agree with Aulén that God often works immediately upon the soul, although he may use various means in the process. There is consequently a mystical element in faith which cannot be denied.

~ Saints ~

The departed saints are essentially in joy because of their direct perception of the glory of God and their abiding vision of God's final and certain triumph.

~ My Vocation ~

I often pray that God might enable me not necessarily to do something great for his kingdom but simply to *do* something, however small it might be. To act out my faith is the goal of my life.

~ The Sexual Life ~

One myth concerning the sexual life is that the suppression of the sexual appetite leads to sexual perversion. Actually it can be demonstrated that the seed bed of sexual perversion is widespread sexual promiscuity. Another myth is that there is a direct correlation between sexual abstinence and sexual abandon. But it has been proved that sexual abstinence weakens the sexual appetite, whereas sexual activity feeds this appetite; and too much sex can make the sexual drive uncontrollable.

~ *The Consciousness of Sin* ~

The one tribulation indispensable to the life of faith is a consciousness of our own sin.

The Christian will always have a consciousness of sin, but this is not a burden, since it is sin that has been forgiven and covered by Christ.

A consciousness of personal sin is necessary to keep us aware of our wretched past, which was forgiven and taken away by Christ, and of the ever-present temptation to return to this past, which can be overcome only through repentance and faith.

Christians cannot be conscious of their sin without at the same time being conscious of their triumph over sin in Christ.

Consciousness of personal sin means consciousness not of the dominance of sin in our lives but of the ever-present threat of sin together with the assurance of victory over sin.

~ *Saints* ~

Baron von Hügel listed the three conditions of sainthood as lifelong loyalty to the faith, heroic action, and radiance. Is not this last condition the one most difficult to fulfill?

~ *Martyrdom and Saviorhood* ~

The deeper significance of Christ's death is not that he was a martyr for righteousness but rather that he was a Savior from sin. He laid down his life not out of devotion to his ideals (although this was present) but as a ransom to evil. He was killed not primarily because of his beliefs but because of who he was—the incarnate Son of God.

1965

JANUARY 1 — MARCH 3

~ *Marriage* ~

The modern view of marriage as the fulfillment of life is idolatrous, since only Christ fulfills life. A marriage in which love and devotion are present can certainly enrich life, but it cannot bring us salvation.

Just as we break the baptismal covenant through mortal sin, so we rupture the marriage covenant through infidelity.

Against the dualistic asceticism that has plagued Christian thought through the ages, I hold that the way to perfection lies not in the renunciation of marriage but in the sanctification of marriage.

The disciple of Christ must never repudiate marriage but may very well forego marriage in order to perform a particular service.

~ Secularism ~

In addition to ultimate and penultimate concerns, there are purely personal concerns. Can it be denied that these personal concerns have crowded out the higher concerns of life?

~ Limbo ~

Those who die in infancy, even if they have been born of Christian parents, do not go directly to Paradise but rather to the World of Spirits where they await the final consummation of all things in Christ. Yet they are taken to a special place in the World of Spirits, which might be called "Limbo," a place where there is no pain or tribulation. The message is preached to them in Limbo, since we are told that Jesus preached to spirits in prison. The reason why infants cannot enter heaven immediately is that faith is the precondition for entry into the kingdom. The error in Roman Catholic theology is to make Limbo an eternal rather than a temporal abode.

~ Nature and Grace ~

Thomas Aquinas held that the wine in Holy Communion is transformed into a pure, angelic substance. Evangelical theology holds that the elements are made channels of the action of the Holy Spirit. In Roman Catholic theology, grace changes or transforms nature. In Evangelical theology, grace uses nature for spiritual purposes.

~ Evangelism ~

Evangelizing consists in socializing and civilizing as well as preaching, since commitment to Christ entails membership in a new society.

The task of the church is not only to bring cups of water to people dying of thirst but to point people to the well, the source of the water. We are sent not simply to serve an ailing humanity but to convert a lost humanity.

~ Christian Mission ~

Our task as Christians is not to reap the harvest but to sow the seed. Yet we should be disturbed if we find that no harvest results from our sowing.

~ Reconciliation ~

Reconciliation is not the absence of conflict but the transformation of it.

~ Jesus Walking on Water ~

Just as the disciples wanted to believe that Jesus did not really walk on the water, that this was only an apparition, so many today would like to believe that Jesus did not really rise from the dead, that his disciples had only a vision of their Master.

~ Retreat Houses ~

There are some who conceive of the retreat house as a workshop for action in the world. Others regard it as a spiritual sanitorium in which we draw near to God in prayer and study. The first group places the emphasis on the practical; the second stresses spiritual renewal. The first group tends to erase the lines between sacred and secular. I would tend to side with the second group but at the same time seek to appropriate the valid insights of the first.

The retreat movement is presently divided into two camps: one is determined to erase the lines between sacred and secular; the other ends in divorcing sacred and secular. Both camps are off-balance. The sacred and the secular are to be distinguished but never separated. In our day when cultural religion is dominant, it would be well to sharpen the lines between church and world while never losing sight of the fact that Christ is Lord of the world as well as of the church.

~ Overcoming Hostility ~

We can overcome the hostility of others by absorbing it, by not allowing it to plunge us into anger or despair.

~ Oxford Group ~

The Oxford Group reminds us that we are called to engage not only in a ministry of the Word but also in a ministry to persons.

~ Bonhoeffer ~

Bonhoeffer rightly reminds us that Christ not only makes us good: he makes us strong. We become not only suffering servants but also warriors of God.

~ Sanctification ~

Calvinism has always talked of sanctification but has given little recognition to the heights of sanctity that are open to the Christian. It sees the Christian as struggling in the valley rather than advancing up the mountain toward the pinnacle of perfection.

~ Prodigal Son ~

It is a mistake to interpret the parable of the prodigal son as
referring to the return of fallen man to God, since the text
clearly indicates that the prodigal son is not an unbeliever but
an errant Christian. An unbeliever is outside the family of
God, for one becomes a member of this family only by faith.

~ Introspection ~

The danger in pietism and its secularized version, group
dynamics, is that we become too immersed in ourselves, and
we thus lose sight of the objective message of the faith. Too
much introspection can prevent us from losing ourselves in
the work and service of Christ.

~ Law and Gospel ~

The Lutheran view is Law-Gospel. The Barthian position is
Gospel-Law. The Calvinist view is Law-Gospel-Law. I am
closest to the last.

~ Birth Control ~

Roman Catholic theologians often liken sex to eating and
argue that the purpose of sex is therefore natural or biological. But do we not eat for pleasure as well as for the
maintenance of life? Is not an important purpose of food the
delight and well-being of humanity and not simply the
physical continuation of humanity? Were not Adam and Eve
told to eat of the fruit in the garden because of the delight
that this would bring them? To be sure, overeating is just as
much a sin as sexual indulgence. But sexual indulgence can
and does take place apart from as well as with contraceptives.

Both Roman Catholics and Protestants formerly argued against anesthesia for childbirth on the grounds that this was against nature and that God intended women to bring forth children in pain. Now many clerics are arguing against birth control for similar reasons.

Just as it is permissible to eat food that has been divested of its nutritional value and therefore does not contribute to the life of the body, so it is permissible in some cases to have sexual relations that are not directly related to procreation.

~ *Baptism* ~

Roman Catholicism holds that baptism by itself effects grace and places an indelible mark on the human soul. Evangelical theology holds that without faith baptism lacks sacramental power and that the regeneration effected in baptism can be forfeited through infidelity to God.

The sacrament of baptism might be likened to an operation. The water is the anesthetic, whereas the actual extraction of the foreign matter is done by the Spirit. The significant point is that the water is a means by which the Spirit accomplishes his work.

~ *Solitariness and Fellowship* ~

One can properly raise objections to both the religion of solitariness and the religion of fellowship. The first type ignores our relationship to our fellowman and the second obscures the vertical dimension of religion. What we need is a religion of fellowship-in-prayer and prayer-within-fellowship.

~ Sacred and Secular ~

In Roman Catholicism the secular is absorbed into the sacred. In liberal Protestantism the secular is practically equated with the sacred. In Evangelical theology the secular is made an instrument of the sacred.

The sacred and secular should be correlated not with church and world but rather with the divine and the human.

The church does not possess a sacred quality as such, but it is the area where the sacred manifests itself.

A Christian should eschew certain secular activities not because such activities are out of bounds or detrimental but because time is at a premium.

~ Saints and Scholars ~

Modern Protestantism upholds the scholar, whereas Catholicism magnifies the saint. It is the person who thinks correctly rather than the person of prayer who is the ideal in Protestantism. We need both the critical mind and the fervent heart, but the latter should take precedence.

~ Sin ~

As Christians we need not fall into sin because we are now united with Christ, but we do fall again and again because of our desire to return to our wretched past.

In the decision of faith we gain full liberation from sin, but there remains in us an aberrant desire (concupiscence), which leaves the door open for our return to sin.

The poison of sin was removed when we were cleansed and baptized by the Holy Spirit, but the wounds from this operation soon begin to fester.

As Christians, we live between the "no longer" and the "not yet." We are no longer in sin, but we are not yet in glory.

Christians are no longer under the power of sin, but they are not yet fully in the domain of grace.

Whereas Wesley insisted upon *posse non peccare* (ability not to sin), Barth speaks of *non posse peccare* (inability to sin) but only as a deed of God, not as a quality of man. Barth holds that only in Christ does *non posse peccare* become a possibility for us, but we fall away from Christ again and again. Does Barth prepare the way for a new understanding of Christian perfection?

~ *Ecumenical Movement* ~

The ecumenical encounter should help us to discern not only the truth in other positions but also the error. We have not made progress in theological understanding if we can only appreciate what others say, holding our critical faculties in abeyance.

~ Salvation ~

We should work out our salvation with fear and trembling, but this is not the same as laboring to earn our salvation.

~ Faith and Reason ~

The Christian faith requires not the abdication of reason but the obedience of reason.

~ Faith and Skepticism ~

The bona fide believer and the cynical rationalist have one thing in common—a distrust of visions and raptures. The believer looks askance at extraordinary experiences because faith has no need of experiential and rational supports. The rationalist is wary of such experiences because they lie outside the purview of reason.

~ Heresy ~

It is better to be heretical yet alive than orthodox and dead.

~ Myth ~

To say that devils enter human beings is metaphorical, for this only describes how we feel something happens. To say that Christ enters human beings is analogical, for this more nearly corresponds to what actually happens.

That Jesus was conceived by the Holy Spirit is a mythopoetic statement. That Jesus had no human father is a literal statement.

~ Pacifism ~

Force can be used to preserve law and order because it is God's commandment that his human creation should live. But force should not be used to crush and enslave humanity, because Christ came that all persons might have abundant life.

~ Philosophy ~

Philosophical systems might be viewed as sacrifices offered to the gods.

~ Gospel and Myth ~

The gospel does not need to be dereligionized or de-mythologized; rather it should be actualized in the cultural situation.

~ Grace ~

Grace is to be understood primarily as the personal favor of God and only secondarily as the effects of God's favor. Moreover, it must be emphasized that the effects of grace in the human soul are dependent on God's personal favor and not vice versa.

My friend and colleague Lee Underhill has sagaciously remarked: "Grace is not an object (a thing); a quantity of merit; or a mysterious fine substance (as in Stoic philosophy and in Tertullian); or a liquid that is infused into the soul to transform it. It is not a quantitative, non-personalistic substance such as water or bread or oil, which communicates a quantitative degree of salvation." Lee holds, as I do, that

God's act of grace is qualitative and personal but that it nevertheless effects an ontological change in man. We are given a new orientation and inward motivation, but our humanity is not mixed or fused with divinity. Rather our humanity is freed from its perversion and distortion.

My friend Father Reginald Masterson recently wrote: "To speak metaphorically, 'The blood of God circulates in our souls.'" However, grace is not a substance but a personal gracious act, which to be sure has physical effects. Human being is never interfused or mixed with divine being, although human being can be said to be grounded in divine being.

Our good works are not simply the byproduct of grace, nor are they the cause of the increase of grace. Rather they signify the working out and fruition of grace.

~ *Demonology* ~

In Christian theology today there are at least five different interpretations of the demonic. Edwin Lewis regards the demonic as an uncreated eternal adversary of God whose work is always negative or discreative. Tillich interprets demons in terms of destructive sociological and cultural forces. Barth understands demons as subpersonal forces associated with the chaos or darkness that has been overcome by Christ; the only power they have today is in the human mind. The animistic or primitive conception, found in some strands of Pentecostalism, identifies demons with disembodied evil spirits that work more or less independently and seek to incarnate themselves in human beings. The Catholic conception, reaffirmed by the Reformers, is that demons are fallen angels under the direction of the archangel Lucifer, or

31

the devil, who exert their power by holding humanity in moral bondage. For at least some of the fathers of the faith, demon possession is not so much being indwelt by an evil spirit as being totally bound to some specific sin or evil. I adhere, with certain modifications, to the Catholic or traditional conception of demonology.

The healing of the Gerasene demoniac (Mark 5:1-20) may be seen as an example of exorcism, but not in the animistic sense. I do not believe that wandering disembodied spirits had incarnated themselves in the possessed man, nor do I believe that they literally entered the swine. It was very probably the demoniac's bizarre behavior that caused the swine to panic and rush into the sea. The words of the demoniac came not from evil spirits but from his unconscious self. The demoniac was undoubtedly in bondage to the supernatural angelic adversary of God. Indeed, his will was no longer his own. He was not actually indwelt by evil spirits that act at random (as in primitive religion), but he was controlled by a superhuman evil intelligence with an overarching strategy and purpose. His deranged personality was rooted in his spiritual bondage, and this is why when his will was freed he was restored to his right mind.

~ *Catholicism and Protestant Revivalism* ~

Despite their obvious dissimilarities, Catholic sacramentalism and Protestant sectarian revivalism have much in common. First, they both believe that regeneration is accomplished all at one time — either in baptism or in the experience of conversion. Again, they both tend to think of the Spirit in terms of an impersonal energy or substance as opposed to a living Subject. Finally, both groups tend to separate Calvary and Pentecost. Catholics speak of the gift of the Spirit being given at Confirmation, the sacrament of Pentecost. Many revivalist groups associate the gift of the Spirit with a second crisis experience after conversion.

~ Gift of Tongues ~

The gift of tongues should be viewed as a steppingstone to a deeper level of faith and prayer. It is a crutch that might be helpful in a certain period of life, but it should be put aside when one commences to walk by pure faith.

~ Communion of Saints ~

The communion of saints differs from spirit communication (as envisaged by modern Spiritualism) in the following respects:

(1) Communication with the saints is always indirect; it takes place through Jesus Christ the Mediator.

(2) Christ alone effects communication between the saints; it cannot be induced by natural means.

(3) Only the eyes of faith can recognize an authentic vision of a departed saint; a true vision is veiled to the senses.

~ True Preaching ~

True preaching is not acting or trying to make an impression; true preaching is pointing to God and his salvation in fear and trembling.

~ Self-transcendence ~

In order to become authentically human one stands in need not of self-realization but of self-transcendence (Frankl).

~ Salvation and Health ~

When one is fully saved, one is completely well. The salvation of the soul entails wholeness in both mind and body.

We can say that one is not fully saved (perfected) without being completely well. At the same time we must acknowledge that one may be truly saved (justified) and yet be sick.

~ Perfect Love ~

Can we love as Jesus commanded us? The answer must be yes and no. We can love with a perfect love because God's Spirit enables us to do so. But we fail to love as he commanded us because we constantly quench the Spirit through self-love.

We as Christians can and do love with a perfect love through the Spirit, but we do not love constantly and fully because we invariably harden our hearts against the Spirit.

~ Faith and Emotion ~

We are called, as Christians, not to give in to our emotions but rather to surrender to Christ. It is incumbent upon us to discipline our emotions, to subordinate them to the mind of Christ.

~ Worship ~

To worship someone or something means to attribute an absolute value to that person or object. We should respect and honor the saints, but we should worship or adore only God.

~ Prayer ~

Prayer is not a means to action but rather the highest form of action. It is not a steppingstone to service in the world but the culmination of Christian service.

~ Active Life ~

What we see today is the active life but not the truly creative life — perhaps because we have lost sight of the dialectic between social participation and contemplation.

~ Sects and Cults ~

A sect signifies an unbalanced emphasis on some tenet of the faith. A cult signifies a basic departure from the foundations of the faith. Both the sect and the cult represent heresy, but the sect can be regarded as an eccentricity whereas the cult is a fundamental aberration.

~ War ~

No war is ever justified in the light of God's strict standard of justice, but some wars are permissible if they serve to preserve or promote a relative state of justice.

1965

MARCH 4 — MAY 26

~ Baptism and Faith ~

It is possible to believe without being baptized, but it is not natural. Faith invariably seeks concrete expression and objective symbolization, for otherwise it is in danger of becoming ethereal and purely spiritual.

~ Tongues Movement ~

The tongues movement today might be understood as an attempt to lay hold of the presence of the Holy, which is missing in mainline Protestantism.

~ Hell ~

The punishment in hell is remedial rather than simply retaliatory. It contains a retributive element, but retribution is made to serve redemption.

Too many theologians today are building houses without basements—that is to say, they are leaving out the doctrine of hell.

Hell as well as heaven is created by the cross of Christ, since only those who reject the cross are consigned to hell.

~ *Saints* ~

A "saint" is not an incarnation of the Holy but a bearer of the Holy.

The Roman Catholic church has preserved the ideal of the saint, which Evangelicalism has lost. But it has recognized only one particular kind of saint—the ascetic.

We should let the light of the gospel shine before others, but we should hide ourselves, our accomplishments and our talents, from others.

The hallmarks of a saint are fidelity, austerity, humility, simplicity, liberality, radiant joy, and love.

~ *Modern Desert* ~

It is possible to speak of the industrial city as the modern desert, for it is here that the principal warfare with the devil will take place.

37

~ Action and Contemplation ~

Contemplation will always bear fruit in action, but action in turn will drive us ever again to contemplation.

~ The Cross and the Blessing ~

Those who are willing to bear the cross but refuse the blessing that accompanies the cross become joyless and despairing. Those who seek the blessing but refuse the cross that accompanies the blessing become empty and disillusioned. We must accept both the cross and the blessing that is given with it.

~ Divine Punishment ~

The suffering that God sends upon us is never retaliatory or purely punitive, but always punitive and remedial at the same time, the latter being the end or goal of the affliction. In God's plan punishment is always made to serve redemption.

God punishes his children in order to correct, restrain, or purify them, not in order to annihilate or ruin them.

We cannot sin against God with impunity; yet God afflicts us only in order to correct and redeem us.

~ Theology of the Cross ~

The words of Elizabeth Clephane's *Beneath the Cross of Jesus* have recently made an impression on me: "I take, O cross, thy shadow for my abiding place; I ask no other sunshine than the sunshine of His face." She is giving vivid expression to the fact that the most authentic theology is the *theologia crucis*.

~ Temptations ~

In the last few years I have had to struggle against two somewhat similar temptations: seeking some extraordinary charism or gift of the Spirit and trying to excel in some form of ascetic devotion. Both temptations were rooted in the sinful desire to make something of myself in the eyes of the world.

~ Experience of the Holy ~

Too many people today try to establish contact with the Holy by rekindling the memory of their conversion experience, but this means that they are no longer directly related to the Holy. What all of us need is a direct and abiding sense of the presence of the Holy.

~ Holiness ~

True holiness signifies wholeness of body, mind, and spirit.

Our standing in the sight of God is not dependent upon the degree of our progress toward evangelical perfection. If this were so, those who have made much progress would become complacent and those who have made little would fall into despair.

~ New Revelations ~

We cannot speak of "new revelations," for God has revealed himself once for all in Jesus Christ; but we can speak of the continuing illumination of the Holy Spirit.

~ Selfless Self-love ~

The Christian life is characterized neither by egoism nor by altruism but by a selfless self-love in that we are to be concerned for our own salvation but only in order to please God and extend his kingdom.

~ Marriage ~

The Catholic church is right to link marriage with fecundity. But Catholic theologians have not fully perceived that fecundity is not only physical but also spiritual.

The purpose of marriage is life-partnership in service and fruitfulness. But fruitfulness must be seen as being spiritual as well as physical.

The purpose of modern marriage is pleasure and companionship. The purpose of Christian marriage is partnership in service and fruitfulness.

~ Communion of Saints ~

The communion of saints might be likened to mountain climbers tied together by ropes. We are advancing upward on Mount Zion, but we can make our ascent only with the help of others.

~ Prayer ~

I am somewhat uneasy about the Jesus prayer in Eastern Orthodoxy and the Rosary in Roman Catholic piety, particularly when such prayers involve constant repetition. True prayer is not a magic formula by which we procure certain dividends or blessings.

~ Withdrawal ~

When trouble assails us we should not seek some special vision or extraordinary sign of God's favor; rather we should retire into a safe place (as did Elijah) until the storm passes.

~ Conversion ~

When we are converted to Christ not only our religious attitudes will change, but also our social and economic attitudes.

~ Peace of God ~

The peace of God is not the contentment of achievement but the knowledge of forgiveness.

~ Conversion in Catholicism and Protestantism ~

The distinction between Catholic and Protestant views on conversion by grace can be made clear by an illustration of a broken-down automobile. In the Catholic conception, the driver needs to have the car repaired and fitted with new parts (infused grace): grace does not annul nature but builds on nature. According to Protestantism, the driver needs a *new* car (a new life): the old nature is crucified rather than remolded or transfigured. Grace contradicts sinful nature: therefore we must be given a totally new orientation or "new being." In the Protestant view, our deliverance rests on our new life in Christ (the new car), but we want to retain our old life (the old car) as well; therefore the old life continues to pose a threat, although in principle it has been abandoned.

~ Final Salvation ~

Before we can enter heaven we must have run the race to Christian perfection, but no one ever makes it in this life to the finish line. We reach the terminal line at death only because this line is brought to us. The crown is given to us despite the fact that we never quite make it to our appointed goal. Our salvation, even our final salvation, is therefore a gift of grace, not a human attainment.

~ Perfection ~

The Christian can have a perfection in intention but not in accomplishment.

The mature Christian may be likened to a mountain climber who is now in the cloud surrounding the upper portion of the mountain. Only when the pinnacle is reached will this person break through the cloud into the light of God's sunshine.

~ Civil Rights ~

I have a suspicion that the church's identification with the civil rights movement today stems not so much from a God-given desire for justice for all as from a sinful desire to win the praise and adulation of the world.

The late entry of the church in the battle for civil rights stems partly out of the penetration of cultural religion into the life of the churches. The church is simply giving its blessing to the cultural aspirations for freedom and equality for all people.

The Spirit of God is certainly at work in the civil rights movement today, since it is God's will that all peoples be free. But the deepest freedom is liberation from sin, and this comes only by the gospel of Christ.

~ *Catholicism and Protestantism* ~

Ida Görres states in her journals *Broken Lights* that she is moving from Catholicism to Catholic Christianity. I can say that I am moving from Protestantism to Evangelical Christianity.

In the Catholic view Jesus stands at the door and knocks, and we proceed to open the door, thereby admitting the Savior into our hearts. In the Reformed view we lack the power to open the door, and consequently Jesus must force an entry into our hearts by breaking down the door.

Our aim in the contemporary Catholic-Protestant dialogue is not to blur distinctions between the two communions but rather to recognize and try to overcome barriers.

43

~ Evil ~

Those who deny the existence of an objective, absolute good are logically compelled to deny the existence of objective evil. Consequently, they are rendered incapable of recognizing and resisting real evil in the world.

~ Sanctification ~

Christians are called not to self-sanctification — attempting to make ourselves holy on the basis of our own resources, but to sanctification by faith — appropriating the holiness of Christ by daily surrender to his Spirit.

The Christian is purified not necessarily at the moment of death but in the transition from death to Paradise.

~ Objective and Subjective Salvation ~

The human condition is that we are dying of an incurable disease — sin. The medicine that can save us has been procured for us by Christ. But unless we actually receive this medicine, we will still die of the disease.

~ St. Mary ~

One of my last books will, I hope, be an evangelical reappraisal of St. Mary, the mother of all Christians.

~ Worship ~

More important than the investigation of the truth of redemption is the celebration of the facts of redemption.

44

~ Eschatology ~

The resurrection of the body and the immortality of the soul (correctly understood) are two ways of describing the same reality.

~ Marriage ~

I am coming more and more to realize that my wife is a gift of God and that my marriage is a veritable means of grace.

~ Demythologizing ~

Our task as Christians is not to demythologize the gospel; rather it is to demythologize the culture in which we live. It is to expose the myths and dreams that modern man concocts to justify his will to power.

~ Our Chief Concern ~

Our chief concern should be not our own sanctity but the glory of God and the advancement of his kingdom. Our efforts should be directed not to self-sanctification but to self-transcendence — being taken up and used by the Spirit of God.

~ Seeking Salvation ~

In seeking our own salvation we should at the same time seek the salvation of others. Salvation is an individual but not a private matter.

~ New Birth ~

In the new birth we do not merely receive new power and energy, but the center of our very being is changed.

The new birth is God being born in the soul. We are still in the birth pangs; our new birth has only begun.

Against the perfectionists we must affirm that the Christian has been reborn not to glory but rather to the hope of glory.

~ Good Works ~

Works of the law are done out of the desire to make ourselves righteous or worthy in the sight of God. Works of love are done out of gratefulness for God's righteousness assured to us by faith in Jesus Christ.

~ Tolerance ~

We should pray to be tolerant of people but intolerant of sin. Moreover, we should be more intolerant of our own sins than those of others.

~ Justification ~

Justification must be operative in sanctification, just as sanctification is anticipated in justification.

We hold to the justification of the ungodly, but only those who seek to become godly reap the full benefits of this justification.

Justification is extended to all but effectually bestowed only on those who believe. It is declared to the whole world but completed only in faith.

~ Word and Life ~

When Paul rejoiced at the preaching of the Word even by preachers whose motives were suspect (Phil. 1:15-18), he was recognizing the fact that only the Word of God, not the Christian life, is indispensable for salvation. Word and life should of course go together, but only the Word is of absolute significance.

~ Theological Themes ~

The theme or motif of Reformation theology is the justification of the ungodly. The theme of Barth's theology is the reconciliation of the world in Christ. The theme of my theology is commitment to Christ in a secular world.

~ Objective and Subjective Salvation ~

By his death Christ opened the gates of the prison in which we find ourselves, but Christ must enter this prison through his Spirit if salvation is to take place.

The event of salvation consists in the conjunction of the opening of the doors to the kingdom and the opening of the eyes of sinful humanity.

~ Salvation by Faith ~

We are *spared* the ultimate torments of sin by the death of Christ on the cross, but we are *saved* from the inner torments of fear and ignorance only by believing in the cross.

~ Puritanism ~

Unlike the Victorians, the Puritans recognized sex as the dynamic and mysterious force that it is. They did not intend to hide or repress the sexual life, but rather to restrain it and direct it according to religious norms. It would seem that we need a renewal of Puritanism today.

~ The Resurrection ~

It is possible to speak of three resurrections: the resurrection to life—at the moment of decision; the resurrection to Paradise—at the moment of death; and the resurrection to final glory—at the end of the world.

~ Faith and Holiness ~

Faith justifies us and thereby entitles us to heaven. Holy love sanctifies us and thereby qualifies us for heaven.

~ *Contributing to Salvation* ~

We cannot contribute anything of our own to our salvation, but we can contribute what has been given to us by God — the graces of a Christian life.

~ *Grace* ~

Grace must be understood not as a power or energy by which we are enabled to become acceptable to God but as the act of God by which we have been made acceptable to him.

~ *Temporal Punishment* ~

The guilt and the eternal punishment due to sin have been removed by Christ in his sacrificial death, but there remains a temporal affliction — the discipline by which God remolds us in the image of Christ.

~ *Faith and Philosophy* ~

The Greeks said "Know yourself." The Romans said "Rule yourself." The Christian faith says "Give yourself."

~ *The Best of All Worlds* ~

This is not the best of all possible worlds because of man's inveterate sin. Yet this world is for the best because of God's infinite love.

~ *Ecumenical Pitfalls* ~

In this ecumenical period we must avoid both the Scylla of doctrinal rigidity and the Charybdis of doctrinal indifferentism.

1965

MAY 27 — SEPTEMBER 13

~ Discipline ~

The disciplined life entails not only disciplined behavior but also disciplined thinking. And this means bringing our reasoning into accord with the Word of God in Holy Scripture.

Christian discipline is not the toilsome, straining, failing effort to be good, but rather the faithful attending on God to receive (Sangster).

~ Fellowships of Renewal ~

What we need today are fellowships oriented about human need, not organizations dedicated to maintaining the establishment.

~ Sin ~

Just as a spider's web will reappear even when a room is periodically cleaned, so social decadence will reappear despite external social reforms. What is needed is the expulsion of the spider, i.e. human sin.

Little children are born not with faith but with the taint of sin. They are claimed by God's love, but this love does not become operative in their lives until their baptism unto repentance.

~ Theological Language ~

Theological language has become devoid of meaning for many people not because this language is archaic (although some of it may be) but because God is withholding his Spirit from a perverse and disobedient people. The language of faith will again become meaningful only when God pours out his Spirit in another Pentecost.

~ Agape and Eros ~

Eros as such can never become agape, but agape can enter into eros and redirect it. Eros and agape sometimes intersect, but they can never become one.

Human love can be so transformed by agape that one can actually love as God loves. Such love can no longer be categorized as eros but is now to be viewed as agape, for it has been taken into and remolded by divine love.

Agape or divine love does not add to or fulfill eros or human love but overthrows and transforms it. This is to say that eros is turned into something other than itself when it is penetrated by divine love. There is no synthesis or correlation between the two kinds of love. We can speak only of the crucifixion and conversion of human love.

~ Spiritual Exercises ~

Spiritual exercises cannot free us from sin and guilt, but they can equip us for service to others.

Spiritual exercises cannot lift us to heaven, but they can strengthen us for service on earth.

As sinners, we cannot reach the heavenly shore by our own labors and ingenuity. Even though this might once have been possible, we now find ourselves in a weakened condition. We must rely not upon our own striving or skill but upon the lifeboat of the gospel manned by Jesus Christ, who will take us to the shore if we will only acknowledge our desperate need for help and accept the free ride to safety. This is to say, we are saved not by our spiritual exercises but by the free grace of God.

~ Salvation ~

The arena of salvation is not the present struggle for social justice but the life of consecration and obedience to Jesus Christ, which may very well entail participation in the battle against injustice and corruption in society. Yet this warfare will be waged with different motivations from those of people of the world and will be directed toward ultimately different ends.

The paradox of salvation can perhaps be made clearer by the illustration of a rowboat in a river that flows into the ocean. As beneficiaries of God's grace, we are placed in the boat and inexorably carried by the current toward the ocean of eternity. It is incumbent on us to row or navigate the boat, but it is the current, not our rowing, that ultimately takes us to our destination. The most our rowing does is to keep the boat in line with the current of the river; it also strengthens us for life in eternity. Yet if we refuse to row the boat, it is in danger of being wrecked on the shoals and jagged rocks of the river. Moreover, there is always the grim possibility that we might choose to row against the current and return to the shore, or even abandon the boat and swim toward what we believe to be safety. We cannot win our salvation, but we can lose it by defying the stream of God's love and abandoning the lifeboat of salvation.

~ The Will to Meaning ~

Most people, if they had to choose between dedicating themselves to something that is true or something that elevates and uplifts them but might not be true, would probably finally choose the former. The will to meaning can be satisfied by nothing else than commitment to the truth.

~ The "God Is Dead" Theology ~

Those who wish to dereligionize the gospel are not radical enough. What is required is to dereligionize the secularistic perspectives of the modern age.

In contradistinction to the "God Is Dead" theology, we must affirm that God is absent, not dead. God is absent because people have become deaf to his Word.

~ My Theology ~

Schleiermacher's theology has been labeled a theology of religious experience. Kierkegaard's can be called a theology of paradox. Barth's is properly designated as a theology of the Word of God. My theology might aptly be termed a theology of Christian commitment.

~ Christian Perfection ~

Just as we can already experience the glory that is to be revealed to us, so even now we function as channels of God's perfect love; but our experience of his glory is fragmentary, and our exercise of his love is imperfect.

A distinction must be made between spiritual maturity and final perfection. The saints in this life can attain a certain degree of spiritual maturity, but they will always fall short of the final or absolute perfection to which Christ calls us.

We can have perfect love in this life but only in an imperfect way. We already taste of the glory that is to be revealed to us, but we have only a first installment of this glory.

Concerning what can be attained in this life, it is better to speak of Christian holiness than perfect holiness, outgoing love than perfect love.

We need to be perfected in holiness before we can enter into the fullness of glory; yet we could not have such perfection unless our glorification had already begun.

~ Gift of Wisdom ~

When I was around eight or nine years of age, I had a vivid experience of God approaching me and offering me any gift that I might desire. I chose the gift of wisdom, for which I have been grateful ever since, though regrettably I have not always exercised it. It is on the basis of the wisdom of God that I now realize that there is one gift that is higher—love.

~ Separation ~

Scriptural holiness means inward separateness but not exclusiveness. Christians are to detach themselves from the values of the world but relate to all kinds of people.

~ Agape and Eros ~

When human love is invaded by divine love (agape), human love must die. But it does not remain dead; it is resurrected as a transfigured human love that now participates in divine love. This is to say, the reborn person now loves with agape.

~ Evangelicalism ~

The label "evangelical" I accept without reservations. Such labels as "mystic," "catholic," "pietist," and "orthodox" I accept only with qualifications.

~ Pietism ~

At the University of Chicago I was a Barthian because the main threat at that time was philosophical theology. Now at the University of Dubuque I have become a "neo-pietist" because the main peril today is cheap grace.

Recently I spoke at a retreat sponsored by the Disciplined Order of Christ in the Deep South. What troubled me at the retreat was the separation of piety and politics, the sacred and the profane.

I am often surprised to find that in pietistic circles many persons are accepted as examples or models who happen to be pious in their actions but are extremely heretical in their beliefs. Yet I am also chagrined to discover that in Christian academic circles many are highly regarded who happen to be proficient in learning but at the same time openly doubt certain truths of the faith and in some cases even live immoral lives.

~ Prayer ~

The worst of all afflictions is the inability to pray.

Prayer changes not only our attitude toward God but also God's attitude toward us. Prayer is able to move the hand of God because God has willed from all eternity to act in and through the prayers of his children.

~ Pentecostalism ~

I am convinced that the success of the Pentecostals in Latin America is due not to their emphasis on tongues but to their ministry of love to the sick, the forsaken, and the poor.

~ Mysticism ~

Against many mystics I affirm that the prayer of supplication must never be set aside in favor of mystical prayer; yet petitionary prayer may very well be supplemented by mystical prayer.

Part of my attraction to such mystics as John of the Cross, Teresa of Avila, John Tauler, and Fénelon is due not to their mystical theology but to their evangelical thrust.

~ Baptism ~

Water baptism might be likened to the anesthetic in a surgical operation and Spirit baptism to the cutting out of the foreign matter from the ailing person. The anesthetic is generally used in a surgical operation, but it is not absolutely necessary.

Like John Nevin, I hold to baptismal grace but not to baptismal regeneration. Regeneration is begun at baptism, but it is realized only in a life of decision.

~ Love and Feeling ~

I have come across this quotation from Charles de Foucauld: "We feel when we suffer—we do not always feel when we love; and this is a great added suffering. But we know that we want to love; and to want to love is to love!" (quoted by Evelyn Underhill in her book *The Mystics of the Church*). This points to the incontrovertible fact that true love, like true faith, transcends experience and that the feeling of love is a fruit of the reality of love, which is hidden even from the self.

Hendrikus Berkhof points out in his book *The Doctrine of the Holy Spirit* that as soon as we try to feel our love we no longer love. He reminds us that love consists primarily in doing rather than feeling.

~ Obedience ~

The proof of faith is not only ethical obedience but also spiritual obedience. The Christian is required to worship God as well as serve humanity.

Wesley spoke of two dimensions of evangelical obedience: works of piety, which concern our duties to God, and works of mercy, which concern our duties to our neighbor. Modern theology speaks much of works of love and mercy but very little of works of piety. Do we not need a more balanced approach today?

~ Means of Grace ~

The Christian is a transmitter as well as a receiver—a channel of redemption as well as an object of redemption.

~ The Saints ~

The saints stand in need of God's forgiveness as well as his empowering grace. They are called not only to serve in love but also to repent.

The life of a saint is characterized by perfection in the sense of spiritual maturity but certainly not in the sense of moral perfectibility.

~ Separation ~

One cannot be a Christian in isolation, and yet one cannot be a Christian apart from a measure of isolation. A Christian must separate from others in order to be alone with God in prayer, but then rejoin others in order to share in the heartaches and glory of the Christian mission.

~ Kierkegaard ~

Kierkegaard reminds us that a church under the cross is characterized not by expansion but by intensity. Its vision is focused not on gaining a place in the world but on preparing for eternity.

Kierkegaard speaks only of the cross of suffering and therefore is compelled to downplay the Old Testament which speaks also of a blessing for this world. The truth is that no cross is ever given apart from a blessing, and no blessing is ever given apart from a cross.

~ Prayer Groups ~

One of my objections to so many prayer groups is that by concentrating on purely personal problems they tend to shut themselves off from the burning social issues of the day. Instead of opening a doorway to the world, they become a means of escape from the real world.

~ Unbelievers ~

Unbelievers will never be citizens of the kingdom, but they will nevertheless be subjects of the king. They will be without the rights and privileges of membership in the kingdom, but they will be beneficiaries of the lovingkindness of the king.

~ Faith ~

Christians must be not only radical believers but also radical doubters. We must doubt every human claim and every creaturely criterion — everything that springs from human wisdom and aspiration. On the other hand, we are compelled to believe, even against our own reasoning, in the truth of faith, for it is implanted within us by God himself.

~ Our Chief Concern ~

I have recently been struck by these words of Scripture: "One thing have I asked of the LORD, that will I seek after; that I may dwell in the house of the LORD all the days of my life, to behold the beauty of the LORD, and to inquire in his temple" (Ps. 27:4). Nothing is said here about mission to the world or the reformation of society, which is now being spoken of in Protestantism as the chief concern of the people of God. Instead, it is made clear that our primary concern should be the contemplation of the glory of God and the searching of his holy will.

~ Sin and Suffering ~

I have recently been helped by a statement of Walter Clyde's (in his *Interpreting Protestantism to Catholics*) that Christians are no longer subject to penalties for their sins, but only to disciplines that enable them to conquer sin. In the Catholic view Christ pays the penalty for Adam's sin, but every person must nevertheless suffer for his or her own sin.

1965

SEPTEMBER 14 — DECEMBER 31

~ Salvation ~

Those who begin to seek for the help of God have already been confronted by the Spirit of God; yet they are not truly saved until they repent and believe. Nor are they fully saved until they go on to perfect love.

The person who begins to seek for help has incipient salvation. The person who repents and believes has present salvation. The person who goes on to perfect love has full salvation.

The saints in Paradise have full salvation, but not until their entry into the consummated kingdom of God will they have final salvation.

The sacrifice on Calvary can be regarded as the objective reality of salvation only for those who have faith. Apart from faith, it is more properly viewed as the objective possibility of salvation.

Karl Heim's metaphor of thunder and lightning to describe the relation of the first and second comings of Christ is not fully accurate, since the second coming is more than a concomitant of the first. It is the culmination and fulfillment of the first.

~ Godliness versus Worldliness ~

Christians are called not to serve the world (as is sometimes contended) but rather to serve God in the world. We are commanded to cultivate not worldliness but godliness in the world.

~ Biblical Inerrancy ~

The Scriptures are inerrant not in the sense that they are wholly in accord with world history and the findings of modern science. Rather they are inerrant in the sense that the writers accurately conveyed and described what was disclosed to them, albeit in the language and concepts of their own culture and time.

~ Death ~

In the Christian understanding, death is not the annihilation or extinction of the self but rather radical suffering and the momentary suspension of consciousness. At death we fall not into nothingness but into the hands of God.

~ Speaking in Tongues ~

Speaking in tongues, like preaching and teaching, is not in itself a work of the Spirit, but it may in some cases be viewed as a human reaction to the work of the Spirit. It can be considered a "gift" only insofar as it enables the recipients to reorient themselves toward life and God.

~ The Locus of the Holy ~

The locus of the Holy is not simply the Word of God understood as a book or even as a message, but the Word of God understood as God speaking to the world today.

The locus of the Holy is neither the Word nor the world as such but rather the Word related to the world, the Word speaking to the world.

~ Biblical versus Popular Religion ~

Biblical faith rests upon confidence in the mercy of God, whereas popular religion is based upon evidences and signs.

Biblical religion is characterized by inward passion and heartfelt trust. Popular religion is characterized by outward observances and uplifting experiences.

~ Murder ~

To kill a person deliberately and with malicious intent is murder. To kill with the intention only of restraining or incapacitating is a tragic accident but not murder.

~ War ~

A state may as a last resort wage war in order to defend the victims of wanton aggression or to secure freedom for the oppressed. And yet in so doing the state is deviating from its legitimate function, which is to preserve and maintain the life of its members. Any war, even a so-called just war, is therefore always questionable in the light of God's law, and the probability is that what begins as lawful killing will end in murder and sacrilege.

~ The Arena of Salvation ~

Against the dominant strand in contemporary "secular theology" I hold that the arena of salvation is not the present struggle for social and racial equality but rather the daily crisis of repentance and faith, a crisis made possible by God's work of reconciliation in Jesus Christ. Such penitence and faith may well entail participation in the battle against injustice and corruption in society. Yet this warfare will be waged with different motivations from those the world understands and will be directed toward ultimately different ends.

~ Baptismal Grace ~

I would not affirm, as some orthodox Lutherans do, that faith is given in child baptism; but I do hold that baptismal grace makes faith possible.

~ Christian Perfection ~

The source of much of the confusion concerning the idea of Christian perfection is that the New Testament word *teleios* can mean both spiritual maturity and ethical perfection. The English word "perfection" includes the meaning of faultlessness, which the word *teleios* does not always imply. We can attain a certain level of spiritual maturity in this life, but moral or ethical perfection is beyond our grasp so long as we remain in this mortal body.

We can attain perfection in the sense of spiritual maturity but not in the sense of moral indefectibility.

The believer can attain a relative or provisional perfection in this life. This is neither perfection in love nor ethical perfection, but rather total dedication to Jesus Christ.

~ *Sainthood* ~

The ultimate concern of the saint is not sainthood but the glory of God. This person seeks sainthood only because it serves the glory of God.

The sinful ego is most virulent when masquerading as a paragon of virtue, as a defender of ideals that are purportedly ethical or spiritual.

Luther has said that there are three types of people — the sensual, the rational, and the spiritual. The sensual person is enslaved by passions. The rational person is caught up in vanity and pretensions. The spiritual person alone is free to serve others with sacrificial love.

~ *Piety* ~

Hand in hand with piety must go morality. We have obligations not only to God but also to our neighbor.

~ *Predestination* ~

Predestination might be defined as *the election of God through the decision of the person of faith.* The decision is not that of the unregenerate person but of the person already touched by the grace of God.

Instead of speaking of double predestination, it is more biblical to speak of a single predestination to life and service for all people. But this predestination is not realized in the same way for everyone. For believers it is realized in their adoption to sonship in the kingdom of heaven. For unbelievers it is realized in their subjugation as servants of the heavenly king.

~ *Paul and Social Action* ~

There are two reasons why Paul did not preach against the social injustices of his time. First, he was living in a totalitarian state where public criticism of the social order meant certain incarceration and even death. Second, he believed that the end of the world was imminent and that we must therefore concentrate our energies on preparing ourselves for the coming kingdom. But because we are not living in a totalitarian state and because we do not believe that the end of the world will necessarily occur in this generation, we must certainly bring prophetic criticism to bear on the wrongs and injustices of our society.

~ *Evangelical Catholicism* ~

Against the world-centered faith of religionless Christianity, I affirm the Christ-centered faith of evangelical catholicism, which is at the same time related to and deeply concerned with the world for which Christ died.

What is needed today is an evangelical catholic pietism as opposed to a sectarian pietism.

My objection to the League for Evangelical-Catholic Reunion is that it tends to put the cart before the horse. We need to arrive at a common understanding of the gospel of redemption before we talk of the corporate reunion of the churches.

~ *Stained Glass Windows* ~

One reason for stained glass rather than transparent windows in a church sanctuary is that the Christian does not have immediate or direct access to the light of God's sunshine and is thereby dependent on the mediation of the Word. A second, more practical, reason is that transparent windows tempt people to look outside.

~ *Christian Unity* ~

Christian unity must be pursued not as an end in itself but rather as a means of implementing the great commission to make disciples of all nations.

~ *Christian Fellowship* ~

The Christian faith speaks not of fellowship per se but of fellowship in service. Its goal is not community as such but rather a common witness to Jesus Christ.

The concern in Christianity is not sociability but a fellowship of love, not togetherness but a community of faith.

~ Biblical Inspiration ~

Inspiration is the divine election and superintendence of particular writers and writings in order to insure a trustworthy and potent witness to the truth. Illumination is the inward awakening of the believer to the truth that is revealed.

Inspiration entails not only the election and oversight of particular writers and writings but also the inward awakening of the company of the faithful to the truth of these writings.

We would have a full definition of biblical inspiration if we understood it as the divine election and guidance of the biblical prophets and the ensuring of their writings as a compelling witness to revelation, the opening of the eyes of the people of that time to the truth of these writings, and the providential preservation of these writings as the unique channel of revelation.

~ Sacred and Secular ~

The relationship between the secular and the sacred should be neither divorce nor identification but rather interdependence.

Harvey Cox maintains that what is needed today is the despiritualizing of the gospel. I maintain on the contrary that the primary need is the desacralizing of secular culture.

The gospel desacralizes the world, but it does not seek the secularization of the world. It sees the world as neither divine nor godless but rather as the theater of God's glory.

~ *Regeneration* ~

Regeneration means that the fever is gone, that the sickness has been eradicated, and yet some of the germs remain. The raging fever may break out again unless we dutifully lay hold of the spiritual medicine of the Word and the sacraments.

~ *Covenant Theology* ~

A covenant theology that holds that children of believers are born into the kingdom promotes the peril of cheap grace.

~ *Mysticism and Evangelicalism* ~

Evangelicalism that is divorced from mysticism becomes rationalistic biblicism. Mysticism that is not integrally related to evangelicalism becomes irrational spiritualism.

There will always be tension between evangelical devotion and mystical spirituality, since the former is grounded in a personal knowledge of God's forgiveness effected in an unrepeatable vicarious sacrifice in history. Yet apart from the mystical element there could be no true Christian devotion. Apart from inner communion with the Spirit of Christ, faith would wither and disappear.

~ *Gospel Preaching versus Ideological Preaching* ~

Gospel preaching upholds the Word of God, which brings all human philosophies and theologies under divine judgment.

Ideological preaching promotes a particular philosophy or value system serving the interests of some social group, which may very well be represented in the congregation. The gospel preacher is a herald of good news. The ideological preacher is a propagandist and apologist.

~ Love and Law ~

The kind of goodness I uphold is neither that of codes nor that of convention but rather that of Christian love, which transcends and at the same time fulfills the law.

The Christian ideal is neither conventional nor codified goodness but rather self-transcending goodness — love that goes beyond the law.

Against the new morality I hold that we are commanded to love not only people but also principles, understood as the law of God — but we are certainly to love people more than principles.

~ Agape and Eros ~

Eros or self-seeking love can be redemptive when purified and redirected by agape or self-giving love. To *seek* union with God and eternal salvation is laudatory when this is done to *give* God the glory.

~ Servanthood ~

Servanthood is to be contrasted not with piety but with religiosity. What is needed is a servanthood in the world that is rooted in a piety not of this world.

Modern secular theology is guilty on two counts: it effectively disengages servanthood from both piety and churchmanship.

~ Gospel Songs ~

We need to differentiate between gospel songs that reflect the tastes of popular culture, such as *Beyond the Sunset* and *Mansion Over the Hilltop,* and songs that popularize Christian truth, such as *Amazing Grace, Blessed Assurance,* and *Wonderful Words of Life.* Certainly we must not throw out all gospel songs.

~ Puritanism ~

In contradistinction to Victorianism, Puritanism combats not sex but sexual license, not the flesh but fleshly immoderation.

~ Prayer ~

In primitive prayer one seeks to cajole and influence the divine power in order to obtain special favors. In evangelical prayer one reveals one's needs and desires to God and then submits humbly to the divine will.

~ Agnosticism ~

Agnosticism is a question mark. Christianity is an exclamation mark.

~ Sanctification ~

I believe not in the sanctification of the perfect or righteous but in the sanctification of the sinner.

~ The Hidden Church ~

Instead of speaking of the visible and invisible church, it would be more proper to speak of the manifest and hidden church. The church is hidden in the visible fellowship of believers, but it is manifest to the world wherever Christians show forth the fruits of the Spirit.

~ Life-goals ~

The aim of the Christian is not happiness but character. It is not freedom from suffering but triumph through suffering.

~ The Vainglory of Life ~

The Christian faith opposes not life but the vainglory of life, not the flesh but the lust of the flesh.

1966

JANUARY 1 — JUNE 12

~ Incarnate Witnessing ~

Just as the Word had to become flesh and dwell among us before we could behold his glory, so our message must be incarnated in the situation of our hearers if they are to know its truth.

~ Free Will ~

The problem of free will might be clarified by the illustration of a sinking ship on the high seas. The passengers have the freedom to move from one deck to another, but they do not have the freedom or power to stave off disaster. The so-called natural man has the freedom to do this or that but not the freedom to save himself from sin, death, and hell.

~ The Demonic ~

The demonic is alien to human nature, but it is not totally alien, since both the human and the demonic reflect the light of God's creation, and in both there is an obscuring of this light.

~ The Church ~

The church might be defined as the fellowship of love centered in the preaching and hearing of the Word of God and the celebration of the sacraments.

The church might be likened to a tree planted in the soil of the living Christ. The tree is dependent upon the soil but not vice versa.

~ Righteousness ~

The "righteous person" as described in Holy Scripture is God-fearing rather than ethically perfect.

~ Billy Graham ~

My objection to Billy Graham's evangelistic crusades is that becoming a Christian is made to appear too easy. Becoming a Christian is not simply a matter of bowing one's head in prayer or going to an inquiry room; rather it consists in a lifelong struggle against the self and the world.

~ The Crisis of Faith ~

The supreme crisis in history is the moment of the incarnation. We become contemporaneous with this moment in faith. Our experience of the moment involves us in a personal crisis that mirrors and rises out of the supreme crisis.

~ Biblical Inerrancy ~

I hold that there is no error in the divine content of Scripture—in its divinely-given teaching and message. Yet this heavenly content is not relayed to us except through the filter of human reasoning that is shaped in part by the vicissitudes of culture and history.

God's Word is without error. But this does not mean that there is no defect in memory, no limitation in horizon, no gap in understanding in the biblical interpreters of God's Word.

The Bible is inerrant with regard to its message, its overall witness to Jesus Christ. It is certainly not free from mistaken notions in the historical and scientific realm. Nor is it free from deficient and sometimes conflicting interpretations in the theological realm, which must be distinguished though never separated from the divine self-interpretation in the sacred history mirrored in the Bible and culminating in Jesus Christ.

~ The Lordship of Christ ~

I agree with Clinton Morrison that we must make a distinction between the lordship and the victory of Christ. Christ is in control of all things, but the present locus of his victory is the community of faith.

A distinction should be made between the universal lordship of Jesus Christ and the kingdom of Christ, which signifies not simply the reign of Christ but the realm where his reign is acknowledged.

~ Reformation and Revival ~

Reformation consists in bringing the organization, the piety, and the doctrines of the church under the criticism of the

Word of God. Revival consists in bringing to life the piety, the institutions, and the doctrines of the church. Reformation entails purification; revival involves restoration. The American church has had many revivals, but it has yet to undergo a genuine reformation.

Billy Graham sees the greatest need today as revival. Secular theologians place the accent on renewal. I see the greatest need as reformation.

~ *Prayer* ~

Prayer that does not bear fruit in service to the downtrodden and outcasts is not Christian prayer but only soliloquy.

Prayer is the highest but not the only form of Christian service. It must never be practiced to the exclusion of works of mercy.

The speaker in tongues utters mysteries unto God (1 Cor. 14:2), but this is not yet conversation with God. Tongue-speech cannot therefore be considered true prayer, although it might be regarded as a preliminary step toward true prayer.

Praying in the Spirit must not be confused with the Spirit praying in us. The Spirit prays in us with sighs too deep for words, whereas we pray in words as we are moved by the Spirit.

77

True prayer is not passive resignation to the will of God but wrestling with his will, even resisting what may be only temporarily his will so that his ultimate will might be done.

In prayer our relations to God are neither exclusively external nor exclusively internal. We are related to the God who stands outside and above us through his Spirit who dwells within us.

Whereas Luther located the source of prayer in the command of God, and Calvin in the mediation and intercession of Christ, my emphasis is on the indwelling of the Holy Spirit.

When we pray for forgiveness in the Lord's Prayer, we pray not simply for deeper assurance of a pardon already given to us but rather that God's forgiveness might be applied to us anew.

In the prayer of adoration we come before God as suppliants, as people who need and seek deeper fellowship with our heavenly Father. Adoration will invariably be followed by supplication, for we ask God to accept our praises.

Prayer is both a means to action and the highest form of action. It is both a steppingstone to service in the world and the culmination of Christian service.

~ *The True Church* ~

I hold the Evangelical Church of the Reformation to be the true church, since it stands squarely upon the foundational truth of the Bible: justification through the free grace of God as revealed and fulfilled in the vicarious, atoning death of Jesus Christ. At the same time, the Evangelical Church is not the whole church or the complete church, since it has yet to appropriate the totality of the authentically evangelical and catholic insights of the church tradition. Nor does it include within its fellowship Christians of other persuasions who emphasize certain truths in the catholic tradition that were neglected by the Reformation.

~ Church Discipline ~

Church discipline is founded on the truth that the church is our spiritual mother and therefore has the right and even the obligation to discipline her children in love. Just as natural parents have the right to exclude the spiteful and disobedient child from family fellowship at the supper table on some occasions, so the church may exclude her wayward children from her fellowship until they acknowledge and confess the error of their ways.

~ Dualism ~

I affirm not an ultimate dualism but a duality within an ultimate unity. I certainly do not hold to the eternal coexistence of two opposing kingdoms — light and darkness. Rather I affirm the eventual and total triumph of the kingdom of light over the kingdom of darkness. Yet there will be some who choose to close their eyes to the reality of this light and who consequently remain in an inner darkness even while they stand in the light.

~ Eastern Orthodoxy ~

It seems that in historical Eastern Orthodoxy the sacred and the secular are practically identified. It speaks of both a holy church and a holy state. This can be dangerous, for it means that the infinite difference between God and humanity is lost sight of, and consequently no judgment from on high can be pronounced on either church or state.

~ *Money* ~

Money can be master, friend, or enemy. For the evangelical, money is a friend to be used for the welfare of others and the glory of God. Luke 16:9 would seem to support the evangelical position.

~ *Two Kingdoms* ~

This world must not be identified with either the kingdom of God or the kingdom of darkness. Rather it is the battleground between these two kingdoms. The victory of God's kingdom is effected only in the community of faith.

~ *Inspiration* ~

I hold that God is the primary author of the Bible and man the secondary author. The biblical writers were limited in their perception of the truth revealed to them, but they were not in error concerning the substance of this truth. They lacked a comprehensive grasp of the mysteries revealed by God, but they did not give a mistaken account of God's will and purpose.

If we hold that God is the primary author of the Bible, we must affirm that the Bible contains the definitive interpretation of God's will and purpose for the world.

~ The Victorious Life ~

It is not innocence but triumph over sinfulness that brings us strength of character.

Only by overcoming shocking sins can we become splendid souls.

~ God as Subject ~

God is not only an object but also a subject, a subject who addresses us from without but who enables us to hear from within by his Spirit.

~ Salvation ~

Catholicism regards the Christian life as a precondition for salvation. Neo-Reformation theology views the Christian life as an effect or fruit of salvation. I understand the Christian life to be a vital element in our salvation, although not its basis or source.

The way to salvation is none other than the *via dolorosa,* the way that led to Mount Calvary. All Christians are called to follow in the footsteps of their Savior.

An escaped criminal who is later found to be innocent still remains in a state of unfreedom until he becomes convinced of his legal innocence. He only becomes free when he is so convinced; otherwise he is simply declared to be free. Christ has freed people from the judgment of hell, but they are not practically and spiritually free until they believe in the saving work of Christ.

Our salvation might be likened to the rescue of a drowning person who has gone under for the third time and can only be revived by artificial respiration. The natural self is dead in sin and needs to be restored to life.

God saves us without our help, but he will not keep us in salvation apart from our cooperation.

Only the person under grace can make a meaningful decision either for Christ or against him. The person who has not been awakened to the significance of Christ can neither accept nor repudiate him.

From the perspective of psychology, our salvation is to be attributed to faith alone. From the perspective of theology, our salvation is to be attributed to God alone.

Our salvation is to be attributed not simply to God by himself but to God in man, to God uniting himself to the man Jesus and to all believers by his Holy Spirit.

Roman Catholics speak of God as the primary cause, and human cooperation as the secondary cause, of salvation. One illustration they give is that of a mother helping her child, just learning to walk, to the door. In my view the child has to be carried to the door against its will.

God's forgiveness is offered to all, but it becomes effective only where there is faith and repentance.

Salvation is fixed at death for those who are in Christ, but the condemnation of those who have never known about Christ is not decided at death.

If we speak of God as the sole cause of salvation, then we must also speak of faith as the sole means by which we lay hold of this salvation.

God effects our salvation without human help but not without human instrumentality.

~ *Children and Salvation* ~

A child of Christian parents is born not into the family of God but into relationship with this family. Although within the sphere of God's grace, the child is not an actual member of the company of the saints until the decision of faith.

Because the speech center in the brain of infants at birth is completely blank and because their cortex is not fully developed, it can be said that infants are not yet complete persons but only individuals. They are able to associate but not communicate. This means that infants cannot yet be considered Christians, although they are already recipients of the love and grace of God.

~ *Sacred and Secular* ~

Against the new secular theology I affirm that the church is called not only to service in the world but also to warfare against the world.

The sacred is not a particular order of existence or activity but a divine Word that stands over against all human existence.

As Christians, we should be both spiritual and secular persons. We should have a hidden discipline of devotion as well as a vocation of service in the world. We fall into sin whenever we seek to be exclusively spiritual or wholly secular.

~ *Social and Personal Gospel* ~

The gospel is both individual and social. We make our decision alone before God, and yet we do not remain alone but take our place as soldiers in the church militant. We enter the kingdom one by one, and yet we are ushered into the glorious company of the saints. We hope for both the salvation of our own souls and the consummation of the kingdom.

We should be concerned with saving souls as well as building the holy community. Both personal salvation and social holiness are necessary in the drama of redemption.

Against a certain kind of introverted culture religion, we must affirm that neither sin nor salvation is wholly individualistic. Sin is rooted in the human person and in society. The salvation of God includes both the individual person and the wider human community.

The gospel we preach is radically individual in that its immediate concern is personal salvation; at the same time, it is unabashedly social in that its ultimate goal is a holy community.

What is needed in the church today is both personal piety and social relevance. Can we have one without the other?

~ The Will of God ~

Forsyth is helpful in his distinction between God's will and his intention. God's ultimate will is life and salvation for all people, but God's immediate intention may be that his children be afflicted so that his final purpose might be realized.

~ Heaven ~

Heaven is not a physical place, but it certainly can be regarded as a spiritual place. To affirm that it is only a condition of the soul or a state of mind is to separate body and soul. Both heaven and hell are dimensions of existence that transcend this present world.

~ The Church and the Kingdom ~

The kingdom is the action that might be likened to drawing a net through the sea (cf. Matt. 13:47-50). It catches not only good fish but also bad, and when the net is brought to the shore, the fish must be sorted out. Entrance into the kingdom means participation in the church; but entrance into the church does not guarantee entrance into the kingdom.

~ The Divine-human Encounter ~

In my theology the divine-human encounter refers primarily to the historic encounter between God and Jesus and secondarily to the inward awakening of believers to the significance of this encounter.

~ The Living God ~

Dr. John Mackay has recently said that instead of speaking of a God "up there" or "out there" or "in here" we should speak of God as "right here." The living Christ stands beside us, guiding us and safeguarding us from all evil.

~ The Holy ~

I maintain that the Holy is to be identified not with works of piety or religion but rather with the Word of the living God that stands in judgment over all human culture and religion.

Against the Roman church, the Reformers contended that the Holy is manifested in both the religious and the common life. They regarded the proclaimed word as the supreme medium of the Holy, and yet they allowed for the fact that preaching becomes a secular or profane activity once it is divorced from the gospel of Jesus Christ.

~ Personalism and Mysticism ~

Biblical personalism should be sharply differentiated from classical mysticism. The biblical prophets, who represent personalism, conceive of faith in terms of personal decision and obedience; the goal of faith is understood as fellowship—with God and the whole company of the saints. Many of the Christian mystics, who have reinterpreted biblical religion in the light of classical mysticism, understand faith as an ecstatic state of self-transcendence and the goal of faith as solitary communion with the ground of being.

In New Testament thought we find not only biblical personalism but also sacramental mysticism. We encounter

God as a Thou who stands over against us, but we also receive the Spirit of God into our hearts through his Word and sacraments. A personalism that is divorced from the Word of God, the sacraments, and the indwelling Spirit soon becomes a kind of philosophical theism. A mysticism that is not directed to God as Personal Spirit soon becomes pantheistic and monistic.

Biblical personalism is as much opposed to philosophical personalism as the Savior mysticism of the Fourth Gospel is opposed to classical mysticism.

~ *Roman and Evangelical* ~

Roman Catholic theology conceives of God as the primary cause of salvation, and human cooperation as the secondary cause. Evangelical theology conceives of God as the sole cause of our salvation, and our obedience as the means by which God accomplishes his saving work. It is permissible in Evangelical theology to regard our obedience as an instrumental cause of salvation, but this does not mean that we play a positive role in procuring our salvation. It means only that we receive it from God and retain it by the power of his Spirit.

~ *The Worship Center* ~

I advocate not the high, towering, enclosed pulpit, which isolates the pastor, but rather a wide roomy pulpit, centrally located and close to the people, in which the pastor has freedom to move about and speak directly to the congregation.

My position concerning the chancel is that the table altar should be out in front in the midst of the people and the pulpit-lectern and the baptismal font should be behind it. This symbolizes the dependence of Holy Communion on both the Word of God and the sacrament of Holy Baptism.

~ Gospel Christianity ~

Gospel Christianity is to be distinguished from every form of eclecticism. This includes an eclectic ecumenism, which seeks an all-inclusive fellowship on the basis of common humanity rather than gospel faith.

~ Evangelical Catholicism ~

Evangelical Catholicism is not Romanism but Gospel Christianity. It is the faith of the Evangelical Reformation applied to the modern situation.

What is needed is an evangelical catholic Puritanism, which seeks purity in worship and doctrine as well as in life.

Evangelical Catholicism is to be distinguished from both Roman Catholicism and an eclectic ecumenical Catholicism promoted by such groups as the League for Evangelical-Catholic Reunion. It is also to be contrasted with Anglo-Catholicism, which signifies simply a return to earlier beliefs and practices.

~ Piety ~

I uphold not a revivalistic but a sacramental piety. It is not the experience of conversion but the nurture of the inner life that should be our paramount concern.

What is needed today is a piety of daily repentance under the cross. Such a piety might be contrasted with the sacramental piety of Roman Catholicism, the experiential piety of fundamentalism, and the social spirituality of secular Christianity.

~ The Devil ~

The devil could not be a deliberate perpetual liar unless he had once known the truth, indeed unless he had once been in the truth. A deliberate or willful liar is one who knows the difference between right and wrong and is therefore not entirely in darkness.

~ Mysticism ~

Heiler maintains that mystics seek exclusive solitude and thereby lack missionary motivation. Yet Catholic religious orders such as the Jesuits and Dominicans have certainly been missionary minded, and these groups are at the same time mystically oriented. The Pietists in the Protestant camp, who have incorporated many of the insights of mysticism, have also been active in missionary work.

There is a mystical as well as a rational element in biblical faith. Yet biblical faith opposes both mysticism and rationalism.

There is a mystical element in Christian faith, but Christian faith is not mysticism. There is also a metaphysical element in Christianity, but Christianity is not metaphysics.

~ *The New Birth* ~

Those who are born but once, die thrice—a spiritual death through yielding to sin; a physical death as a consequence of sin; and an eternal death as the final judgment on sin. Those who are "born again," die twice: a death to sin in the decision of faith; and a physical death as a reminder of the sin that has been overcome.

I believe Tillich is correct when he says that the new birth does not make us new beings but rather places us in a new reality that can make us into new beings.

~ *Biblical Personalism* ~

What is needed today is a piety grounded not in religious enthusiasm but in biblical personalism.

My position might be categorized as a biblical personalistic evangelicalism as opposed to a conservative rationalistic evangelicalism.

~ *Ecumenism* ~

Secular ecumenism seeks the functional unity of Christians in order to perform common tasks in the world. Churchly ecumenism seeks the organizational merger of churches into one all-inclusive church with a common confession and witness. Spiritual ecumenism seeks the spiritual unity of Christians for the purpose of inter-church cooperation in social action and evangelism. Evangelical ecumenism seeks the spiritual and visible unity of Christians for the purpose of the conversion of the world to the gospel of Jesus Christ.

~ Justification ~

Justification must be viewed as both extrinsic and intrinsic. It is a declaration of righteousness and an impartation of righteousness.

I uphold not extrinsic justification understood as a juridical act of God occurring wholly outside of us, but rather extrinsic-intrinsic justification, allowing for both the declaration and the impartation of righteousness.

Luther sometimes fell into the error of interpreting justification as wholly extrinsic to humanity. Yet he did not remain in this error, for he acknowledged in both his early and his later years that the *imputation* of righteousness invariably involves the *impartation* of righteousness.

~ The Fall of the West ~

The three stages in the disintegration of the modern world can be seen in the movement from relativism to nihilism to diabolism.

~ The Saints ~

By abandoning the doctrine of the saints, Protestantism has been unable to combat the modern adulation of the hero.

~ Heresy ~

Most heresies do not actually state that which is erroneous but that which is defective. They affirm only a part of the truth rather than the whole counsel of God.

~ Worship ~

Two things trouble me about contemporary Protestant worship: the disappearance of charismatic preaching and heart-felt singing.

~ The Norm of Love ~

I hold that the final norm for faith is not simply love but the living Word of God, which unites love and truth.

Whereas Paul Ramsey reduces Christ to a principle of love, Barth sees the commandment fulfilled by a Christ who loves and who calls us to bring our action into accord with his love.

The Puritans acknowledged the overriding importance of both divine love and divine justice. Social Gospelers preached primarily about social justice. Some of the new secular theologians see the hope of the world in a universal, authentically human love.

~ Bearing the Cross ~

Bearing the cross is not the same thing as bearing burdens. No one can escape burdens, whereas the cross can be avoided. One is conscripted to carry burdens, but one must volunteer for the cross.

~ The Cross of Christ and the Christian Life ~

The cross of Christ is the foundation, cause, and prerequisite of the Christian life.

~ Neo-evangelicalism ~

My theology could be described as a type of neo-evangelicalism, but one that appeals to Catholic tradition as well as to the Bible.

~ Biblicism ~

Biblicism regards the Bible as a definitive and absolute authority in and of itself. The Reformation position is always the Bible united with the Spirit; never the Bible standing by itself.

~ Inspiration ~

Inspiration might be defined as the divine election and guidance of the biblical writers and the ensuring of their witness as the unique channel of revelation.

~ Need for Withdrawal ~

What is required today is a more radical detachment from the world if there is to be a deeper penetration into the world.

~ The Criterion for Ethics ~

I reject the idea that there is one kind of ethics intended for believers and another for unbelievers. The criterion for ethics is the gospel together with the law, which is implanted to some extent in all human beings but is explicitly revealed in the Decalogue. God's law is binding on all people, but only Christians are enabled to understand it fully and only Christians are empowered to obey it.

Against contextualist ethics I affirm that the divine criterion, the Word of God, which brings us a new vision and new power, rises above as well as includes the context in which we find ourselves.

~ *The Spiritual and the Temporal* ~

I maintain that the kingdom of God is a spiritual kingdom, but this does not mean that it has no relationship to the world in which we live. It is spiritual because its origin and goal are located in the transcendent realm. And its power and blessings are derived from that realm. On the other hand, the kingdom of God is present in the world as an alien but at the same time vital force seeking the conversion of all peoples to Christ. This mission not only entails the conversion of souls, but it may also involve the reformation of social structures. The kingdom of God is a spiritual community, but it is a community that has temporary residence in this world, and therefore it has a very real concern for this world. Moreover, this world is the arena in which the kingdom of God advances against the powers of darkness. The weapons by which it advances, however, are primarily spiritual, not temporal, and the goal toward which it moves is also essentially spiritual. The world as such will never be brought under the dominion of the kingdom of God but will forever be a battleground between light and darkness.

The mission of the church has both a spiritual and a temporal dimension. We are called to commit ourselves to the kingdom that is not of this world, but we are also summoned to minister and witness in this world.

The church can realize its spiritual mission only as it is involved in the agonies and conflicts of this world.

The church has a divine message, but it must be incarnated in the language of this world in order to bear fruit. The church has a spiritual mission, but it must be related to the agonies of this world if it is to be actualized.

The church has a spiritual message — but with far-reaching social consequences.

If Christ is Lord of all, we must acknowledge his commandments in every sphere of life. Our secular as well as our religious activities must be brought under his judgment.

1966

JUNE 13 — DECEMBER 31

~ Conservative Evangelicalism ~

I am both a conservative and an evangelical, but I do not identify myself with "conservative evangelicalism" insofar as this entails a belief in biblical literalism and inerrancy.

~ Catholicism and Protestantism ~

It is important to understand that Evangelical worship is based on the grateful acknowledgment and proclamation of the sacrifice of Christ, not the offering of this sacrifice.

Against the League for Evangelical-Catholic Reunion I hold that what is needed is not a return to Rome but a return to the gospel.

The bane of Catholicism is a sacramental objectivism. The bane of modern Protestantism is an experiential subjectivism.

We should aim not for the synthesis of Evangelical and Roman Catholic thought and practice, but rather for their mutual purification in the light of the Word of God so that what is authentically evangelical and catholic might come to the fore.

~ Humanization ~

I agree with the secular theologians that salvation entails humanization. But I contend against these men that the ground of humanization is divine justification. The horizontal relationship of human beings to one another is based on their vertical relationship to God.

~ The Good Samaritan ~

At a Salvation Army service in Rockford recently, I heard a fresh interpretation of the Good Samaritan (Luke 10:25-37). This story presents us with three opposing philosophies of life. The motto of the first is, "Stick them up and take what is theirs." This view is exemplified in the robber who waylaid the traveler to Jericho. The second philosophy says, "Pass them up and keep what is yours." This view is exemplified in the priest and the Levite who ignored the wounded stranger on the road. The third philosophy says, "Pick them up and share what is yours." This view, the Christian view, is exemplified in the Good Samaritan who bound up the wounds of the stranger and took him to the inn.

~ Faith and Justification ~

Whereas Barth maintains that the subjective apprehension follows the objective event of justification, I believe that the objective occurrence and the subjective apprehension are two sides of the one event of justification and that neither has effect apart from the other.

In my view, faith is not subsequent to justification but concomitant with justification.

~ *The Mission of the Church* ~

When I say that the mission of the church is to save souls, I mean that it is involved in the restoration of human beings — not only to spiritual salvation but also to health and wholeness. The church should be concerned with the social as well as the spiritual welfare of humanity.

The mission of the church has both a spiritual and a temporal focus. It proceeds from the spiritual (the church) to the temporal (the world), and then from the temporal to the spiritual (the kingdom).

The mission of the church is essentially but not exclusively spiritual.

The mission of the church is directed to the world but also beyond the world to the kingdom. Its origin and goal are to be located in the spiritual realm, but its immediate reference is the temporal realm.

It is the task of the church to bring the spiritual to bear upon the secular, rather than escape from the secular into the spiritual.

Our mission stems from the spiritual, but it is in and for the temporal.

The church should not engage in partisan politics, but it should be intimately concerned with political issues that are at the same time moral issues.

In a time when religion is becoming increasingly confused with politics, we need a theology of the inner life. Indeed, before we can relate ourselves intelligently to the world of politics we must be in a right relationship with God.

The Christian message has reference to both this world and the next. It is directed to people in this world in order to prepare them for the world to come.

The mission of the church is essentially spiritual—to herald a kingdom that is not of this world. At the same time, this spiritual mission has far-reaching implications for life in this world.

The mission of the church is to minister to people in this world as well as to prepare them for the world to come.

~ *Worship* ~

Most people come to church to be instructed, challenged, entertained, or informed. But true Christians come to church to give glory to God.

~ Resurrection of Jesus ~

The resurrection of Jesus does not mean that he returns to earthly life but rather that he is raised to spiritual life.

~ A Theology of Devotion ~

The old liberalism placed the accent upon the image of God in humanity. The old orthodoxy stressed the sinfulness and helplessness of humanity. A theology of evangelical devotion emphasizes the new birth and the indwelling of the Spirit.

Twenty years ago what was needed was a theology of crisis to remind Christians of the critical turning point in history—the death and resurrection of Jesus Christ. Now the crying need is for a theology of devotion to urge Christians to respond to what God has done for us in Christ.

The alternative to secular theology is a theology that stresses heartfelt devotion to Jesus Christ—not merely in the context of worship but in the context of daily life.

Just as Pietism saved the church in the seventeenth and eighteenth centuries, so "evangelical devotionism" is needed to save the church in our time.

I prefer the term "devotionism" to "devotionalism" because my stress is on commitment and consecration rather than on worship as such.

For secular theology the key word is *identification*. For the evangelical theology I propose, the key word is *devotion*.

My theology of devotion differs from fundamentalist pietism in three ways: it is ecumenical rather than sectarian; it holds to a dynamic rather than a static concept of revelation; and it is oriented about the life of obedience under the cross rather than the experience of salvation.

The answer to the secularization of the church today lies neither in renewal activism nor in restorationist biblicism but rather in evangelical-catholic devotionism.

Unlike the Pietists, I emphasize not the possession of salvation and the joys of the heart but rather the struggle to retain salvation. The theme of my theology is not the experience of conversion but the life of obedience.

An evangelical theology of devotion places the accent not on the assurance of salvation but on the working out of our salvation in fear and trembling.

An evangelical theology of devotion is to be contrasted with revivalistic fundamentalism by its emphasis on a life of obedience under the cross rather than on a crisis experience of conversion.

The roots of a theology of evangelical devotion lie not in revivalistic fundamentalism but in historic Lutheran and Reformed Pietism and the catholic evangelicalism of the Protestant Reformation.

~ The Trinity ~

The three-in-oneness in God is analogous to water, steam, and ice.

~ *Grace and Free Will* ~

Catholic theologians sometimes give as the example of the role of free will in salvation a mother leading to the door her little child, who is just learning to walk. A better example from my point of view is a mother who takes her ailing child, kicking and screaming, to the operating table where the root of the affliction is extracted. The natural self needs to be cleansed of sin and born again before it is possible to walk in the light.

~ *Sin in Christians* ~

As Christians we are no longer in sin, but sin is still in us. Therefore even Christians stand in need of repentance and conversion.

~ *Hell* ~

God presently forsakes and abandons those who reject Christ, but he will eventually take even these to himself.

Christ came to save us not from oppression and persecution, but from hell.

~ *Sacred and Secular* ~

Our task as Christians is not to sacralize the profane but to turn the profane toward the sacred. It is not to transform the profane into the sacred but rather to ground the profane in the sacred.

The ultimate loyalty of the church is to its spiritual Lord, but its immediate concern is the agonies and needs of the secular world.

When everything is sacralized then nothing is sacred, since the root meaning of sacred is being set apart from the profane.

The church is called to sanctify but not to sacralize the secular. The secular remains secular, but it is made to redound to the glory of God.

The spiritual order refers to our relationship to God and also our relationship to our neighbor in and through God. The secular order refers to our relationship to the world without direct reference to God.

~ *Need for Withdrawal* ~

Too many Christians have lived in the smog-blanketed city of the world for so long that they have tended to forget that there is such a thing as pure air. What Christians need is periodic withdrawal into the hills so that they can get clean air in their lungs and then return to the city with a renewed vision, determined to be smog fighters.

~ *Personal and Social Salvation* ~

The church should be concerned with both social problems and personal sins, since it seeks a holy community as well as individual salvation.

We are called to social as well as to personal perfection. This means that we should strive for a holy community as well as individual salvation.

~ *Lord's Supper* ~

We must avoid both a crass materialism and an ethereal spiritualism in our theology of the Lord's Supper.

Theologians (both Catholic and Protestant) are too much concerned about the change in the elements in the Eucharistic celebration. What is just as important (if not more so) is the inward change, the change in the hearts of believers, manifested in contrition and repentance.

~ *Sacraments of Initiation* ~

It is interesting to note that the Catholic church regards baptism, confirmation, and the Eucharist as sacraments of initiation. This implies that the baptized infant is not yet fully in the church.

~ *Billy Graham* ~

We must thank God for an evangelist like Billy Graham who has led tens of thousands of lost souls to a saving knowledge of the Lord Jesus Christ. Graham's crusades are not beyond criticism, but his positive contributions are a blessing to the church.

~ Revelation ~

In divine revelation the Spirit of God imparts to people of faith conceptual knowledge, but it is the responsibility of the faithful to translate this knowledge into affirmations that can give objective guidance to the church. Yet our propositional statements are at least one step removed from the revelation itself and therefore always stand under the judgment of revelation.

There is an inseparable connection between the revealed Word of God and the Bible, but not an absolute identity. God's Word cannot be frozen in the pages of Scripture, just as it cannot be packaged by the clerics of the church.

~ The Indwelling Christ ~

I maintain that although all people are in Christ in the sense that he is the Representative of all, it does not follow that Christ is in all people. He died *for* the whole human race, but he dwells only *in* believers.

~ Baptism of the Holy Spirit ~

The truth in the charismatic revival is that even after baptism by the Holy Spirit, believers still need to be filled with the Holy Spirit.

The Spirit could not be given until Jesus was glorified because the pattern in spiritual power had to be fixed.

The two signs of the baptism of the Holy Spirit are purity of heart and the power to witness.

The converted person has already been baptized by the Holy Spirit but must still be anointed and filled with the Spirit.

Those who stand in need of the baptism of the Holy Spirit are those who are only nominal Christians, whose new birth has been aborted. And this may well include the great majority in our churches today.

The baptism of the Holy Spirit can occur more than once in the life of the baptized; if one has totally fallen away from the faith one needs to be engrafted into the body of Christ a second time.

~ Faith and Signs ~

Bultmann emphasizes that faith can have no empirical or experiential supports. He urges us to walk by faith instead of seeking signs. Yet does he not ignore Jesus' words that no sign shall be given *except* the sign of Jonah — the resurrection on the third day?

~ Weak Faith ~

It is customary in many circles to speak of inactive members and inactive faith. Faith can be weak, but it can never be inactive. The trouble with our churches today is that they retain on their rolls persons who are not converted and who ipso facto are not Christian.

There can be weak faith, but not partial faith. There can be faith that wrestles with and overcomes doubt, but not faith that is partly doubt.

~ Nature and Grace ~

Grace not only restores us to essential manhood but also raises us to Godmanhood.

Against Roman Catholicism I contend that God does not alter or change nature but rather uses nature as it is.

~ Original Sin ~

Original sin is not simply weakness but a besetting weakness. It is not merely lust but a lust for power.

~ Word and Sacrament ~

The fact that both Jesus and Paul hardly ever baptized, yet constantly proclaimed the kingdom message, points to the priority of the Word over the sacraments.

~ Favorite Hymns ~

Three hymns that accurately reflect my theology are: *In Thy Service, Lord of Mercy* by Ewald Kockritz; *In Thy Service Will I Ever,* translated by Carl Philip Spitta; and *I Will Sing the Wondrous Story* by Francis Rowley.

~ Repentance ~

I have a distinct remembrance of the first time I repented of my sins. I was but a small child. The occasion was a book of short stories for children on moral truths. I wept profusely and had to seek the solace of my mother, who assured me that my sins were indeed forgiven.

Today, Aug. 28, 1966, I have been overwhelmed by such a deep conviction of sin that for more than two hours I have been placed in a state of sorrow erupting into tears. This sin is not imaginary: it concerns my prideful insistence on my own way these past two weeks at our vacation home in Michigan. How it is possible that sin still retains such a hold on me is difficult for me to fathom.

There is only one thing worse than refusing to repent, and that is repenting without being serious about changing one's life.

~ Two Types of Freedom ~

It is well to distinguish between spiritual and natural freedom. Spiritual freedom is the freedom to hear and obey God, and this is none other than salvation. Natural freedom or free will is only the freedom to choose between alternatives that are open to us in our fallen state. Natural freedom is a sign of both our original paradise and our present bondage.

~ Forgiveness ~

We can speak only of an offer of forgiveness when considering the salvation procured for us by Christ. If forgiveness is to be actualized, it must be accepted as well as offered.

~ Kerygma *and* Didache ~

The *kerygma* must not be understood as the "all" of Christianity but rather as the beginning of it. The *didache* is also included in the canon of faith.

~ *Virgin Birth* ~

The main reason for the Virgin Birth is not that Jesus had to be born sinless or that this proves his divinity, but rather that God chose to use this particular means to incarnate himself as a sign to the church of the supernatural origin of Christ.

~ *Doctrine and Life* ~

Doctrine apart from devotion is empty; devotion apart from doctrine is blind.

~ *Marriage* ~

Because of the gift of a lovely wife, I am coming again to believe in the goodness of creation.

When a man is in his wife's arms, he should not try to think of the transcendent. But when he is in the arms of a mistress or prostitute, he would then do well to think of the transcendent—indeed of the coming judgment of God.

~ *Situation Ethics* ~

After reading Fletcher's *Situation Ethics*, I can only conclude that this is an ethics of prudential calculation, not of evangelical obedience.

~ Pornography ~

I would define pornography as any talk or writing that degrades human beings, that incites to sexual perversion. Given this definition, it would seem that the state has an obligation to bar such material from children and adolescents.

~ Sex ~

The answer to the dehumanization of sex is not its divinization but rather its humanization.

~ Death ~

Death might be compared to an anesthetic that God administers to the soul in order to prepare it for a new body.

~ The Norm for Christian Life ~

Some Christians are lukewarm; others are feverish. The norm is Jesus Christ, who was authentically human and whose life contained both balance and ardor.

~ Two Types of Piety ~

The piety of total surrender is illustrated in Wesleyanism. The piety of daily repentance under the cross is to be found in the Protestant Reformation.

~ Spiritual and Material ~

The Christian religion represents a synthesis of the spiritual and material in that the Word became flesh. Yet the spiritual has priority over the material, since the Word became flesh so that flesh might be transformed into spirit.

In Christianity the material is to be utilized, not idolized.

~ The Need Today ~

What is needed today is not a return to the monastery but a breakthrough into a new form of Christian discipleship — pioneering fellowships of renewal.

~ Justification of the Sinner ~

God accepts us even while we are sinners, but he does not continue to accept us if we remain in our sins.

~ Hallmark of the Gospel Minister ~

The true minister of the gospel is neither a salesman nor a showman but a spokesman.

~ The Two Dangers ~

We must be on guard against both the biblicists and restorationists on the one side and the renewal activists on the other.

~ Religious Communities ~

An evangelical religious community would be founded not on the principle of acquiring holiness but on the principle of availability for service.

~ *Thought and Action* ~

The one who thinks but does not act is ineffective; the one who acts without thinking is dangerous.

~ *Pietism* ~

In Pietism the new birth means peaceful possession, enjoyment of salvation. In the evangelical theology I espouse, the new birth involves a decisive commitment to the will and work of God.

The Pietist concern is personal edification. My concern is obedience under the cross.

The Pietist emphasis is on the joys of the heart and the possession of salvation; my emphasis is on a life of sacrifice and perseverance.

~ *Life and Doctrine* ~

Sound doctrine apart from a holy life is intellectualism; a holy life apart from sound doctrine is moralism.

~ *Dogma and Doctrine* ~

I agree with P. T. Forsyth that "dogma" should be restricted to the "irreducible Gospel." Dogma is "final revelation in germinal statement." Doctrines are truth about dogma—dogma expounded.

~ *The State as a Kingdom* ~

"Kingdom" as it appears in the New Testament has a spiritual connotation. A secular state is a governing community that should be concerned primarily with the preservation of law, order, and justice in the world. It is not a "kingdom" that calls for absolute loyalty and obeisance.

~ *Eternal Life* ~

The primary focus of the gospel is not on abstract eternity but on eternal life, which is partially realized and appropriated in the travails and encounters of this life.

~ *Mysticism and Evangelicalism* ~

My affinities are more with radical evangelical theology than with Christian mysticism.

~ *The Decalogue* ~

The Decalogue is inseparable from but not identical with the Word of God. As it stands it reflects the cultural limitations of the Jewish ethos. But when it is united with the law of love, it becomes absolute truth.

~ *Religious Experience* ~

Religious experience must not be seen as a substitute for revelation; it is rather the means by which we appropriate revelation.

~ Saints ~

There are some would-be saints who seek to do *every* lowly task and are resentful when others also try to serve. Such persons are not saints but proud sinners who seek their own honor and elevation in lowly service.

~ Unbelief ~

It is a mistake to regard the unbeliever as a prodigal son. He is rather a son of darkness even though he was created to be a son of light. What he needs is not to return to some hypothetical original status but to be converted to a new status.

~ Call to Perfection ~

Christ calls us not to a relative perfection (which would be imperfection) but to absolute perfection, and this is precisely why we can never be perfect in this life.

~ Transcendence of God ~

The Christian God is neither "out there" nor "down here" but "over here and there."

~ Secular Theology ~

Secular theologians speak of the need for new forms of witness and service. But the still greater need is for new persons.

~ *Christian Liberty* ~

Christian liberty is not transcendence of the law but loving adherence to the law (cf. Ps. 119:44-45).

~ *Objectification of God* ~

The existentialists are right when they maintain that we cannot objectify God. But they fail to recognize that God can and does objectify himself.

~ *The Taboo Today* ~

The one subject that is totally taboo in our society is neither sex nor death but divine judgment and hell.

~ *Need for Prophets* ~

We should be not children of the times but rather prophets to the times.

~ *"Brotherhood of Man"* ~

The Christian is not a brother but a friend of all humanity. Only Christ can make people brothers and sisters by adopting them into his kingdom by means of the gift of faith.

All people have a common Creator, but only Christians have a common Father.

~ Death of Christ ~

Christ's death was not in vain—even for the world of unbelief. He died for the salvation of believers and for the condemnation of unbelievers. His death determines the destiny of all people, but not in the same way.

~ Mission of the Church ~

Our lives are to be centered in God but to be lived out in the squalor of the world in his service.

~ Two Types of Love ~

The all-inclusive love of agape, which includes love *to* the self, should be distinguished from the radically exclusive love of eros, which consists primarily in love *for* the self.

~ Biblical Inspiration ~

To speak of God as the primary author of the Bible does not mean that God dictated the actual words to the biblical writers. Rather it means that he selected and sanctioned their words as the vehicle of his Word.

The Bible comprises both wheat and chaff. The chaff, however, is not outright falsehood but that which is peripheral and nonessential in the Bible. It is the covering in which truth is concealed. The chaff becomes error only when it is mistaken for the wheat.

When I say that the Bible contains chaff as well as wheat, I mean that there are parts of the Bible that are marginal and peripheral — but certainly not worthless.

~ Faith and Experience ~

Just as life does not come from oxygen but there must be oxygen for life, so faith is not derived from experience but experience is a necessary medium of faith.

~ Biblical Inerrancy ~

The concept of biblical inerrancy is ambiguous because no one has yet given a satisfactory statement of what this means. If it means that the world view of the writers is in full accord with the facts of science, then the Bible is certainly not inerrant. But if it means that the writers faithfully recorded what the Spirit enabled them to discern, then the Bible is inerrant.

~ Biblical Authority ~

The Bible's authority must be based not on the debatable premise that it contains no historical inaccuracy or deficient theological formulation, but rather on its capacity to render a reliable and trustworthy picture of God's dealings with sinful humanity.

There is sufficient mystery in the Bible to confound the expert and sufficient clarity to convert the sinner.

~ *Biblical Interpretation* ~

Biblical interpretation is more like building with blocks than putting together a jigsaw puzzle. Our task is not to make every part of the Bible fit into a harmonious whole; rather we are called to build upon a firm foundation. If we build upon the solid rock, the gospel of Jesus Christ, then every part of the Bible becomes significant, even though the full picture is not yet within our grasp.

~ *Organization in the Local Church* ~

A local church should have only four groups, each oriented about one of these themes: evangelism, Christian service, prayer, and social action. These groups moreover should be open to all members—young and old, single and married.

~ *Faith and Mysticism* ~

Faith consists not only in mystical participation but also in personal confidence. Consequently we can speak of both a Savior mysticism and a biblical personalism.

~ *Supernatural Creationism* ~

I hold neither to monism nor to dualism but to supernatural creationism. God is not the sum total of reality, nor is there a second reality coeternal with God. Rather God created a reality apart from himself, which continues to exist only by his will.

~ *The Demonic* ~

The devil still has a kingdom, although it has been driven underground and has no legal status.

~ *Breaking the Law* ~

Jesus broke the law from above it. The two thieves broke the law from beneath it. All three were crucified at Calvary.

~ *Transcendence of God* ~

The god of deism is wholly transcendent. The god of pantheism is totally immanent. The god of panentheism is basically immanent, though open to transcendence. The god of Christian faith is basically transcendent, but he is also radically immanent.

~ *Sin* ~

Sin is not a *deprivatio,* the loss of something good, but a *depravatio,* a wicked corruption.

~ *Kingdom of God* ~

The kingdom of God is not only "beyond history" but also "in the midst of us" (Luke 17:21).

~ Piety ~

Piety consists not so much in a feeling of absolute dependence (as Schleiermacher held) as in repentance and obedience under the cross.

~ Worship and Service ~

Prayer to God should take precedence over service to our neighbor, but when our neighbor is in immediate danger God tells us to cease praying and go to our neighbor's aid.

Loyalty to God takes priority over love to our neighbor, but when our neighbor is in immediate danger, out of loyalty to God we must desist from specifically religious duties and go to our neighbor's aid.

~ Salvation, not Solutions ~

Modern theologians do not seem to understand that people today, as in every day, cry not for solutions but for salvation.

~ Spiritual Bondage ~

Such disorders as alcoholism, homosexuality, dope addiction, and kleptomania must be understood not merely as sicknesses but as forms of spiritual bondage. Only divine grace can ultimately break the shackles that bind people to these vices.

It is fallacious to hold that alcoholics, dope addicts, criminals, and sexual perverts are not morally responsible.

Their bondage is not a physical incapacity but a spiritual incapacity. They are slaves to evil because they willfully submit to evil. They must therefore be held accountable for their misdeeds, even though their will is in captivity.

~ *"Man Come of Age"* ~

If our ultimate goal is power, then modern man has come of age. But if the goal is the meaning of ultimate existence, then man has descended to a new infancy (Abraham Heschel).

~ *General Presence of God* ~

It is better to speak of a general presence of God in the world rather than of general revelation, since God can be present without necessarily disclosing himself.

~ *Sacramental World* ~

We must be cautious in speaking of a sacramental world, because the world is under the dominion of the power of darkness and is no longer inherently receptive to divine grace.

~ *Mysticism* ~

The mystical experience apart from Jesus Christ is an encounter with nothingness.

~ *Personhood* ~

To be a person is to be capable of being addressed by God, and this means to be able to hear and understand God's Word. An infant is an incipient person, but not yet a person in the full sense of the word.

~ True Peace ~

True peace is not the absence of conflict but the presence of God.

The peace that Christ gives is not the absence of conflict but stability amid tension.

~ Overcoming Anxiety ~

The surest way to overcome anxiety is to risk one's reputation, even one's life, for the sake of the kingdom of God.

1967

JANUARY 1 — AUGUST 31

~ *Prayer* ~

In evangelical prayer we do not passively resign ourselves to God's will; rather, we actively seek to discover God's will in heartfelt supplication.

In evangelical prayer we submit ourselves to God's will only after great agony and questioning. We do not simply abandon ourselves to God's will.

We wrestle with God not for the purpose of making him kind or generous but rather to gain his attention and make known to him the extremity of our need. He already knows our needs, but he wishes us to come to a full realization of these needs before he deigns to act to fulfill them.

~ *Self-denial* ~

We must not depreciate ourselves but seek to keep ourselves from all evil. We must not renounce our talents and gifts, but at the same time we must beware of seeking to use these to enhance ourselves.

~ Anthropology ~

The human person is not a rational being predisposed to good but an emotional being predisposed to evil.

The curse of humanity is not the outer tragedy of fate but the inner tragedy of guilt.

~ Doctrine of God ~

The world reflects the glory of God, but it is not to be viewed as the mask or body of God.

God is not the non-objective but rather the trans-objective. He is in and above the world of objective reality.

A liberal preacher said recently that we need to take God out of the attic (meaning the heavens) and bring him down into the living room of humanity. But this God is still confined in the house of humanity. The true God towers above and beyond the domain of humanity, although he enters this domain time and again.

~ Sanctification ~

God loves us as we are, but he wants us as he is.

Sanctification refers to the change in the character and personality of the human person, which is only initiated in the experience of faith.

Because saints are still sinners, they need to be ever watchful against temptation.

~ *Fundamentalism and Liberalism* ~

We need to move beyond both the literalistic approach of fundamentalism and the historical-critical approach of liberalism to the pneumatic post-critical approach of catholic evangelicalism.

The fundamentalist has his heart in the right place but not his mind. The extreme liberal has both mind and heart in the wrong place.

Whereas fundamentalism may be said to be characterized by rigidity, liberalism is marked by anarchy. One can get angry at fundamentalists, but one can only pity liberals.

~ *Salvation* ~

Our salvation takes place not only on the cross but also in the church. It depends on the living Christ active within his church as well as on Christ crucified.

The paradox of salvation is being completely subjected to God, yet wholly free.

The Christian is truly *saved* from sin but is never entirely *rid* of sin in this life.

We are saved *by* personal faith, but we are saved *in* the company of the faithful.

Salvation entails a change of character as well as a change of status. It signifies a new being as well as a new relationship.

~ Growth in Knowledge ~

Christians need to grow in both knowledge and discernment (Phil. 1:9), and this means testing everything in the light of the Word of God.

~ Conscience ~

There are two ways to cope with a guilty conscience. One is to calm the conscience by repenting of sin. The other is to kill the conscience by denying the reality of sin.

~ Theology ~

We should *glance* at the great theologians, but we should *gaze* only at the Savior, Jesus Christ.

~ Two Kingdoms ~

The state is an institution ordained by God to protect the rights of the individual and maintain order in society. It is not a kingdom that can demand the veneration of people. When it pretends to be so, it becomes demonic.

~ *Kingdom of God* ~

The kingdom of God is not the reign of God over the whole world but the rule of God in the hearts of believers.

~ *Fear* ~

We take ourselves too seriously because we do not take God seriously enough. We are prone to be fearful because we have not placed our fear in God.

~ *Sex* ~

The Christian faith teaches not the denial of sex but the subordination of sex to the goal of kingdom service.

Sex is neither dirty nor divine, but it can become an instrument of self-will or of outgoing love.

All erotic attraction must not be categorically identified as lust. If it is controlled and directed by agape love, then it certainly is not sinful.

~ *Ecumenism* ~

True ecumenicity springs not from disloyalty to one's confessional tradition but rather from fervent loyalty to what is essential in one's own tradition.

Theology today is faced with three alternatives—the liberal, the sacramental, and the evangelical. In ecumenical circles there is much talk about the first and second, but the third is practically ignored. Yet can there be an ecumenical theology unless it is solidly evangelical as well?

~ Fundamentalism and Liberalism ~

Fundamentalism represents the narrowing and confinement of evangelicalism; liberalism presages the dissolution of evangelicalism.

~ Conservative Evangelicalism ~

My quarrel with conservative evangelicals is that they tend to see revelation as wholly objective rather than objective-subjective. Revelation does not happen unless we are inwardly illumined by the Holy Spirit so that we can grasp the significance of the biblical testimony.

~ Church and World ~

What is needed today is not only to get the church back into the world but also to get the world out of the church.

We need to get the world out of the church so that the church will be free to challenge the world.

~ The Devil ~

The devil died in the eighteenth century; God died in the nineteenth century; man has died in the twentieth century.

The demonic does not signify the absence of light but the obscuring and discoloring of light.

The demonic is not simply the negation of the divine; rather it participates in a distorted way in the holiness and power of the divine.

~ *Asceticism* ~

In a dualistic asceticism one seeks to crush the body in order to save the soul. In evangelical asceticism one seeks to restrain the body in order to save both body and soul.

In evangelical asceticism the purpose is to deny not so much bodily appetites as self-will, but this entails restraining the body.

~ *Evangelism* ~

Apart from the good news, our good works are ineffectual for the salvation of others.

We are called not only to accept Jesus Christ as Savior but also to follow him as Lord in active obedience.

Evangelism seeks to bring about not only commitment *to* Christ but also commitment *through* Christ to ministry in the world.

~ Mission of the Church ~

We are called not only to make converts but also to make disciples, which means teaching people to observe all the things Christ has commanded.

The church should be concerned about improving the human lot as well as changing human nature, since Good-Samaritan service is an integral part of its ministry.

The church needs to rediscover its spiritual mission but without abrogating its responsibility to speak to the crucial issues of our time. Indeed, if the church is truly focused upon the commandments and promises of God revealed in the Bible, it will be moved to bring the gospel to bear upon the whole of society, including political and economic life. But it must beware of identifying God's Word with any social program or political crusade, because this would mean a capitulation to secularism.

~ Doctrine of Scripture ~

We must make a distinction between what Scripture teaches and what Scripture reports. Scripture reports many things that are in error, but its teaching, i.e. its message, is inerrant.

I hold that the humanity of the authors of Scripture was not merely an instrument but a medium of the Word of God, and therefore we do not have this Word in its original and unadulterated form.

Those who champion the doctrine of biblical inerrancy make faith dependent upon the latest findings of biblical criticism. For it is only the critics and scholars who can determine whether the Bible is totally inerrant.

I prefer to speak of the infallibility rather than the inerrancy of Scripture. Infallibility is a religio-confessional term, whereas inerrancy is a scientific-apologetic term.

Roman Catholics hold that the message of Scripture must be interpreted by the church, but the deeper truth is that this message is interpreted by the Spirit to the church.

The Bible is a revelation not only of God's person but of God's truth.

The Bible is not only illumined by the Spirit but also corrected by the Spirit (with regard to the formulation of truth). Fundamentalists have not an open but a closed Bible in that they do not allow for this kind of correction.

The Bible is inerrant in what it purports to say concerning God's revelation, not in what it inadvertently says on matters of science and history.

Scriptural inerrancy can be affirmed if it means the conformity of what is written to the dictates of the Spirit concerning the will and purpose of God. But it cannot be affirmed if it means the conformity of all that is written to the facts of world history and science.

131

~ Personal and Social Salvation ~

One of my basic criticisms of the tradition of revivalism is that salvation is described solely in terms of individual decision, and the need for believers to affiliate themselves with the community of faith is regarded as a secondary matter. We are never saved in isolation but always in relation to the church, the body of Christ.

We believe by ourselves but not for ourselves or unto ourselves. Our faith cannot exist in isolation but must actively seek the good of others.

The Christian religion is personalistic but not individualistic. We must personally respond to the gracious initiative of God, but our response has no lasting efficacy except in the community of faith.

~ Spirituality ~

Spirituality might be defined as the attempt to strengthen and live out one's relationship to the divine.

Evangelical spirituality seeks to bring the whole person—including the full range of secular activities—into relationship with God.

Spirituality refers to the dimension of one's relationship to God, particularly to activities intended to deepen this relationship.

Spirituality means life *with* God and *for* God rather than the attempt to make oneself worthy in the eyes of God.

Spirituality means surrender and dedication to God rather than trying to make something of oneself before God.

Spirituality concerns our relationship to God and how it can be deepened.

The proper object of spirituality is not humanity as such but humanity in relationship to God. It is not the spirit of humanity so much as the Holy Spirit working in humanity.

~ *Spiritual and Secular* ~

We as Christians are called to give away our cloak as well as our faith. But the two are not the same, and the latter is certainly more significant.

Christians will be both spiritual persons and active participants in the secular world. Our ultimate concern will be the service of the glory of God, but we are also to have a lively interest in the society in which God has placed us. We will not necessarily repudiate the goods of this world but seek to use them for the glory of the kingdom. We will be open to the secular but not immersed in the secular. We will be concerned for the secular but not bound to the secular. We must live and work in the world but take care not to become secularized, i.e. preoccupied with the things of this world. We are to accept the world as God's creation but renounce the love of the world, which is the hallmark of secularism.

Devotion to the sacred involves not contempt for the secular but rather gratitude for the secular.

It is impossible for Christians to become disenchanted with the world, because they have never been enchanted by it. They never despair of the world because they do not live by the standards of the world.

We like to speak today of the Word becoming flesh and dwelling in our midst. Yet we also need to stress the complementary truth that Christ rose from the grave and ascended into heaven.

~ *Evangelism* ~

Two things are necessary for successful evangelism—love for persons and zeal for the truth.

Proselytism is manipulation and treating persons as objects; evangelism is witnessing in love.

~ *Justification* ~

We are justified even though we are sinners, not because we are no longer sinners.

Works do not play a role in the cause of justification, but they are a factor in the implementation of justification.

The act of justification occurs simultaneously with the commencement of regeneration; the process of regeneration is the evidence and confirmation of our justification.

~ Regeneration ~

Regeneration is both a finished work in the past and an ongoing process. Our inner renewal takes place in the decision of faith, but it must continue throughout life.

I believe that in the decision of faith our carnal nature is crucified, not eradicated.

It is possible to say too much about conversion and also too little. We say too much when we regard the convert as fully regenerate. We say too little when we imply that regeneration has not really taken effect.

Just as natural birth comprises a series of stages including conception, gestation, and delivery, so regeneration or the new birth may also be divided into stages.

Our regeneration begins when we seek for Christ by the prompting of his Spirit; it is completed when we commit ourselves to Christ in the power of his Spirit.

~ Regeneration and Sanctification ~

Regeneration means entering upon a new existence; sanctification means becoming conformed to the Incarnate One.

Regeneration means entering upon a new existence; sanctification means developing a holy personality.

Regeneration means being engrafted into Christ; sanctification means being conformed to Christ in life and work.

In pietistic circles, regeneration is often viewed as a state of being and sanctification as a process. But then we lose sight of the biblical truth that the Christian is only partly in Christ and needs to put on the new nature ever again.

Regeneration can be understood as participation in Christ, being engrafted into Christ; sanctification connotes obedience and conformity to Christ in life and work.

The relationship between regeneration and sanctification can be illustrated by the case of a man stricken with paralysis, who is placed on the road to recovery by a potent drug. He must now exercise constantly in order to build up his body, but he always needs fresh doses of the drug if life is to be sustained. Having been regenerated we must go on to sanctification, but we also need to return constantly to the wellspring of regeneration in order to gain power to continue our pilgrimage.

~ *Christian Love* ~

Such verses as Luke 14:26 and Matt. 10:37 definitely indicate that we are to love Christ more than our fellowman. Indeed, we are called to adore Christ, whereas we are forbidden to adore our fellowman.

It is well to bear in mind that the commandment to love was addressed to the disciples of Christ. This commandment makes no sense to non-Christians, since for them Christian love is an impossibility. But Christians are enabled to love because they are indwelt by the Spirit of God.

Love does not necessarily mean wanting to be in the company of others but rather willing the good of others.

~ *The Holy* ~

The Holy is the transcendent presence of Christ in the midst of his people.

No part of the being of the Christian ever becomes the Holy, but every part of the life of the Christian should be directed by the Holy.

~ *Regeneration and Sanctification* ~

In regeneration one's nature and horizon are changed; in sanctification one's personality and character are changed.

The inward change — regeneration — does not take effect upon human personality all at once but rather throughout life. The progressive change in personality — sanctification — is the result or outcome of the inward change.

137

~ Morality ~

One should have moral indignation but not moral pride. One should have spiritual fervor but not spiritual pretension.

~ Naturalism and Supernaturalism ~

The demythologizers have rightly urged us to abandon the three-story universe of primitive mythology. But they have substituted a one-story universe, which is equally untenable.

~ Important Books ~

I have been influenced in my theological development by three important books: *The Cost of Discipleship* by Dietrich Bonhoeffer; *Commentary on Romans* by Martin Luther; and *Prayer* by Friedrich Heiler. A book that I have just finished reading, P. T. Forsyth's *The Church and the Sacraments*, is also likely to leave an indelible impression on my theology.

P. T. Forsyth's writings have revived and strengthened my conviction of the truth of the evangelical position.

~ Incarnation ~

The deepest meaning of the Incarnation is not that the Word was made flesh but that the Holy was made sin for us.

~ *Sin and Sickness* ~

Sin might be likened to a gust of wind that shakes an apple off the tree. Sickness might be likened to the rot that sets in as the apple lies on the ground. Sin, which separates us from our source of sustenance, is the presupposition of sickness and death.

~ *Evangelical Devotion* ~

The direction of my theology is away from mystical spirituality and toward evangelical piety.

Whereas liberalism placed the accent upon the fatherhood of God and neoorthodoxy upon the cross of Christ, a theology of evangelical devotion gives primary emphasis to the gift of the Holy Spirit.

In evangelical theology the Spirit of God enables us to see not the glory of God but our own sins.

There will always be tension between evangelical devotion and mystical spirituality. First, unlike mysticism, evangelical devotion is anchored in an unrepeatable historical event—the sacrifice of Jesus Christ. Second, evangelical piety is oriented about personal fellowship rather than union with the undifferentiated ground of being. Third, this kind of piety is based on the message of the justification of the ungodly, which is incomprehensible to most mystics.

~ Justification and Sanctification ~

We are not justified *by* a Christian life, but we are sanctified *through* a Christian life.

~ Faith and Experience ~

Faith is not a sixth sense but rather the divine light that informs all our senses.

Religious experience might be likened to drinking pure water drawn from a well. The water (salvation) is not derived from our experience, but it is mediated through our experience. Its source is the well (the living God). It is made available to us through the pipes and the glass (the Bible and preaching). But unless we actually drink of the water from the glass, we do not yet have salvation.

~ Sin ~

We have been endowed with a will to live, but in our sin we have transmuted this into a will to power.

~ Baptism of the Spirit ~

Many church members are not yet Christians but pre-Christians. They are seeking for salvation, but they have not yet made a decision for Jesus Christ. They have been touched by the Holy Spirit but not baptized by the Holy Spirit.

~ Spiritual and Secular ~

One thing I admire in the Salvation Army is that it holds onto the secular mission of the church as well as the spiritual gospel.

~ Faith and Works ~

Faith apart from works is religiosity; service apart from faith is do-goodism.

It is better to have no belief in God and yet to do works of mercy than to believe and to do no works of mercy. And yet salvation eludes us until we are grasped by a living faith that issues in works of love.

~ Reason and Revelation ~

The truth of revelation cannot be fully appropriated by reason, but reason can be molded and redirected by revelation.

~ Secular Theology ~

I agree with the secular theologians that human rights come before property rights, but I insist that God's Word takes precedence even over human rights.

1967/1968

SEPTEMBER 1 — MAY 31

~ Gospel and Social Reform ~

The church should seek to deal not so much with the symptoms and manifestations of sin as with sin itself. It should concern itself not so much with social amelioration as with personal regeneration through the cross of Christ.

Too many church people today are expending their energies in improving the social environment of the prodigal son instead of calling him back to his Father.

Today we seem to be more concerned about the social environment and personal comfort of the prodigal son than about his estrangement from the Father in heaven.

It is appropriate for the church to suggest directions for public policy, but not to offer "directives."

~ Sex and Religion ~

We who are practicing Christians can have the assurance that our sex life is also acceptable to God not because lust is totally absent but because our sins are covered by the righteousness of Christ.

The Christian faith does not repudiate the pleasures of the flesh but only such pleasures as are unlawful. At the same time, it esteems much more highly the pleasures of the spirit.

The Christian neither divinizes nor repudiates sex but rather subordinates it to a higher goal.

~ Justification and Sanctification ~

Justification deals primarily with the guilt of sin; sanctification deals with the pollution of sin.

~ Biblical Authority ~

I affirm that the message of Scripture is infallible and that the Spirit infallibly interprets the message to people of faith. But the inerrancy of the letter of Scripture is not an integral part of the Christian faith.

Because of the ambiguity of the term *inerrancy,* I hold that it is better to speak of the *veracity* of the Bible.

The prophets and apostles bring to us not only the divine perspective but also their cultural inheritance. We have the divine message only through the instrumentality of a particular history and culture.

The Bible is both divine truth and human testimony. Liberals recognize the second aspect and fundamentalists only the first.

It is not the text of the Bible that is infallible but the teaching of the Bible.

~ Sanctification ~

It is not so much the exercise of spiritual gifts as the ripening of spiritual fruit that is the evidence of sanctification.

We are called not simply to mature manhood but to Godmanhood.

It is well to note that sanctification has a double meaning: being set apart from the world and being purified from sin. Both these elements are neglected in present-day theology.

~ The Christian Life ~

We should be in the world but not of the world. We should live in the flesh but not according to the flesh.

In much Protestant piety after the Reformation, sanctification follows regeneration: we are called to grow in the faith that becomes ours in the moment of decision. I hold that we must not only grow in faith but also return ever again to the Giver of faith. We need not only to repent of our sins when we are first confronted by the cross, but also to repent daily under the cross.

~ Holy Spirit ~

Those who have been baptized as infants but are without faith can be said to have the Holy Spirit *with* them but not yet *in* them.

In order to grow, a plant needs not only sunshine but also water or else it will wither away and die. So a Christian needs not only the light of God's Word but the presence of God's Spirit in order to grow into maturity.

It is theologically more sound to speak of a twofold blessing of the Spirit than of a first and a second blessing. Both justification and sanctification are given to us in the moment of faith.

~ Regeneration ~

We are incorporated into Christ in a moment, but we are not transformed in a moment.

For the original Pietists regeneration meant incorporation into Christ. For the later revivalists it signified instant transformation.

145

Regeneration is a crisis that might be likened to the apex of a pyramid. There is a line leading up to it and a line leading down from it. No crisis in the life of the soul is a single point. It is the pinnacle of a pattern of experience (from the book *Like A Strong Wind Blowing*).

I am coming more and more to regard regeneration and sanctification as two dimensions of one salvific process that has a definite beginning point. Our inner renewal begins in a particular moment, but it must continue throughout life.

Regeneration consists not in the alteration of the old nature but in the impartation of a new nature.

Regeneration has occurred once for all in the life of every Christian, and yet it continues on a new level.

The desire for rejuvenation in modern culture reflects the new pagan mood, which is to be contrasted with the Christian emphasis on rebirth.

~ *Fundamentalism* ~

Modern fundamentalism is distinguished from classical orthodoxy at two points. First, it tends to regard the Bible alone rather than the Bible with the Spirit as divine revelation. Second, it champions the inerrancy of the Bible in matters of history and science, whereas the older orthodoxy for the most part was content to uphold the Bible as infallible in faith and morals.

~ *Catholic Renewal* ~

The present renewal in Roman Catholicism probably has its source in the Renaissance conception of autonomous person-hood rather than in a rediscovery of the Word of God in Holy Scripture. But this is not to deny that the Spirit of God can also work through secular movements.

~ *Humility* ~

Humility is not to be confused with a feeling of inferiority. Humble people can face the future with confidence, since their trust is not in themselves but in the living God. People who feel inferior are unable to draw upon a source of strength beyond themselves and are therefore vulnerable to all kinds of doubts and fears. Both humble people and those crippled by a sense of inferiority are conscious of their defects, but the former are also aware of the forgiveness and love of God.

~ *Grace* ~

It is theologically more accurate to speak of grace as inexorable rather than irresistible in that grace triumphs even where it is resisted.

~ *Defense of Religion* ~

We need to take seriously Toynbee's warning that the defenders of religion in their attempt to stifle fanaticism have too often extinguished faith.

147

~ Justification ~

The final justification will be according to our works. But it is important to understand the nature of these works. The question that will be directed to those who are disciples of Christ is whether they have openly confessed their faith in him (Matt. 10:32-33) and have been obedient to the will of the Father (Matt. 7:21-23), persevering in faith to the very end (Mark 13:13) and also showing to others a forgiving and merciful spirit like that shown to them (Matt. 18:23-35). In other words, the works by which they shall be judged are none other than the evidence of a living faith (a paraphrase of Philip Watson, *The Concept of Grace*, p. 40).

~ Eschatology ~

I affirm not the doctrine of a second chance for salvation after death but the universality of a first chance. Those who were unable to hear the gospel in this life will surely be given such an opportunity in the World of Spirits.

We may hope for the salvation of all people, but this is not an article of faith.

Against Moltmann I hold that the eschaton does not mean the merely future but the absolute future as opposed to history.

~ Holy Spirit ~

There are four basic emotions associated with receiving the Holy Spirit: joy, love, sorrow, and fear. We have joy because of sins forgiven; we have love because Christ first loved us;

we have sorrow out of a conviction of sin; we have fear because we acknowledge Christ as Lord as well as Savior.

~ *Holiness* ~

Today we need a holiness in the world, which is quite distinct from the unholy this-worldliness of secular theology and the "aholy" otherworldliness of mysticism.

~ *Evangelical Christianity* ~

The evangelical principle is not the sacrifice that God demands but the sacrifice that God becomes.

We need to move beyond the rationalism of the older orthodoxy and the mysticism of existentialist theology to the personalism of evangelical, biblical faith.

Evangelical theology places the emphasis upon the message of justification by the free grace of God revealed in Christ — the message declared in Holy Scripture and received by faith alone.

An evangelical is neither a rationalist nor an irrationalist but a fideist, that is to say, someone who tries to live and walk by faith alone.

~ *Otherworldliness* ~

Just as there is a false otherworldliness disdainful of life in this world, so there is also a true otherworldliness that gives

149

significance to life in this world. The first type is mystical and gnostic; the second type is biblical.

~ Revelation ~

Divine revelation signifies not simply event + interpretation but rather event + interpretation + inward illumination.

The Word of God is not a timeless truth but a personal address. It is not an eternal idea but the movement of God into human history.

~ The Christian Task ~

Our responsibility is to rest in Christ, and then he will work through us. We are called first of all not to work but to trust.

Our goal should not be to make God more real to people, since only God can accomplish that. Rather we should confess the distorted reality of our lives and acknowledge that God alone has eternal reality.

~ Demonology ~

One possible explanation of the demons entering the swine in Matt. 8:31-32 is that the devil unveiled himself to these animals and thereby drove them into panic.

~ Holy Communion ~

This evening (Feb. 20) our seminary celebrated the service of Holy Communion according to a new experimental liturgy.

Because I was not convicted of sin, I did not partake of the elements. If one is not convicted of sin, then Communion becomes only another form of cheap grace.

~ Gospel and Social Reform ~

We need to bear in mind that the gospel gives the ultimate solution to the human predicament, not penultimate solutions. It does, however, throw light upon approximate or penultimate answers and thus contribute indirectly to social reform.

~ Divine Grace and Human Love ~

In one sense human love and fulfillment precede divine grace, since one cannot hear or understand the gospel unless one knows in some small way what it means to care and to belong. At the same time, human love does not make one willing or ready to receive divine grace. Human love is a precondition for understanding the gospel proclamation but not for believing in it.

~ Limited Atonement ~

The atonement of Christ is intended for all people, but it secures the salvation only of some. Yet this is due to unbelief in the human heart, not to a decree of God that rules out part of the human race beforehand.

~ Sin and Salvation ~

The Holiness churches remind us that the Christian has the ability not to sin, though not the inability to sin.

Those of us who are in the church must see ourselves first as Christians and only second as sinners. If we view ourselves primarily as sinners, we are in danger of denying the reality of divine regeneration.

When we give our hearts to Christ, the curse of sin is taken from us, but in its place is put the cross of faith.

Our age is characterized by the death of sin rather than the death of God. We need not so much a new conception of God as a renewed conviction of sin.

~ Cheap Grace ~

Evangelical indicatives must always be combined with moral imperatives if we are to avoid the peril of cheap grace.

~ My Vocation ~

I am coming more and more to understand my calling as being in the direct service of the gospel. Some seek to uphold Christ through social service, which is a worthy vocation, but I am called to proclaim Christ in a direct manner.

~ Christian Freedom ~

Christian freedom does not mean freedom to negate the law but freedom to apply the law to the concrete situation in which we live.

~ Evangelicalism and Biblicism ~

In our criticisms of existentialist theology we must beware of returning to rationalistic biblicism.

We must avoid the errors of both a biblicistic rationalism and a subjectivistic experientialism if we are to present an evangelical theology anchored in Scripture and relevant to the needs of our time.

~ Prayer ~

Prayer brings healing as well as meaning to our lives. Through prayer we not only come to know God's will, but we are also penetrated by the divine presence.

~ Sin and Anxiety ~

I must disagree with Shestov that anxiety presupposes the loss of freedom, since on occasion Jesus was anxious, though always free from sinful bondage.

A distinction should be made between being mastered by anxiety and tempted by anxiety. Jesus was tempted by anxiety, but he never succumbed to it; rather, he triumphed over it.

~ Contemplation ~

Evangelicals are prone to be spiritual activists. Liberals tend to be social activists. What is needed in Protestantism today is more contemplation.

~ Secular and Sacred ~

The secular should be understood neither as a substitute for religion nor as its enemy but rather as its field of action.

~ Two Kingdoms ~

The two-kingdom theory of Luther should be reappraised rather than abandoned. There *are* two dimensions of reality, the spiritual and the temporal, and these should not be confused even though they cannot be separated.

The two-kingdom idea is often expressed in our worship services by the two flags on either side of the chancel representing church and state. But a much more appropriate symbolism is the state flag under the church flag. The kingdom of God is above and within the kingdom of the world.

The truth in the two-kingdom theory of Lutheran orthodoxy is that there is a qualitative difference between the spiritual and the temporal, the sacred and the secular. This truth must not be lost sight of as we seek to reinterpret the two-kingdom concept for our time.

~ Sainthood ~

The marks of saintliness are reverence toward God, severity toward self, and tenderness toward others.

~ Evangelical Revivalism ~

I have often wondered why so many children of those who stand in the tradition of evangelical revivalism rebel against the faith of their fathers and mothers. Can it be that these children were looked upon by their parents as less than Christian, indeed even enemies of God, because they lacked the experience of conversion?

We must not only lay foundations for faith but also build on these foundations. Revivalists tend to stress the first without giving due consideration to the second.

~ Degrees of Sin ~

Bonhoeffer rightly reminds us in his *Ethics* that there are heavier sins and lighter sins. A falling away is of infinitely greater weight than a falling down.

~ Confessing Church ~

The need today is for a confessing church rather than a merely confessional church, a living faith rather than a lifeless creed.

~ Oases of Spiritual Life ~

Oases of spiritual life have become a necessity in the modern desert of secularism and nihilism.

~ Marriage and Celibacy ~

The man or woman who chooses celibacy over marriage may have a practical advantage but certainly not a moral advantage.

~ Faith and Love ~

Fénelon refers to both love without feeling and faith without seeing. This is permissible provided that we go on to affirm that love, like faith, has concrete effects upon our senses and that both love and faith may at times arouse our feelings.

~ Faith and Philosophy ~

Classical philosophy begins in wonder. Existential philosophy begins in despair. Christian faith begins in obedience.

~ Faith and Experience ~

Experience plays a decisive role wherever there is faith in God. When God encounters us, we experience his presence. When God withdraws himself, we experience his absence.

~ Spiritual Disciplines ~

Dr. Nels Ferré has rightly warned against the tyranny of sleep and has strongly encouraged the spiritual discipline of early rising.

~ Favorite Hymns ~

Among gospel songs that have become favorites of mine are *At Calvary* and *Amazing Grace.*

~ Doctrine of God ~

The God of the Christian faith is neither "amorphic" nor anthropomorphic but theomorphic. He might also be described as theanthropomorphic—God with man and God in man.

~ Fall of Man ~

The fall of man as recorded in the Bible is prehistorical rather than ahistorical. It is saga rather than myth.

~ Human Misery ~

We are created for love but are corrupted by self-love—this is the key to our misery.

~ Significant Books ~

Within the past few months two books have made a deep impression upon me: *Athens and Jerusalem* by Lev Shestov and *The Theology of Jonathan Edwards* by Conrad Cherry.

~ Infallibility of the Church ~

The infallibility of the church rests primarily in its Lord and Head, Jesus Christ, and secondarily in its sacred book, the Bible.

1968

JUNE 1 — DECEMBER 31

~ *Preparation for Salvation* ~

The following should be distinguished: reprobation, preparation, and regeneration. Those in the second state are seeking
for salvation, but they are not yet effectually converted.
They may assent to the faith intellectually, but they have not
yet been baptized with the Holy Spirit.

Puritan theology reminds us that there is a preparation
for salvation prior to the reception of salvation. Yet we must
insist that this is not a legal preparation but an evangelical
preparation; it is an integral part of the work of salvation
itself.

~ *Baptism of the Spirit* ~

Those who begin to seek salvation can be said to be moved by
the Spirit and even empowered by the Spirit, but they are not
yet baptized with the Spirit. Their new birth is set in motion,
but it has not yet been actualized. They are on the threshold
of salvation, but they are not yet fully saved.

I agree with the Pentecostals that church people today stand in need of the baptism of the Holy Spirit, but I insist that this is none other than effectual conversion to Jesus Christ.

Those who were baptized with water before Pentecost can be said to have been guided and moved by the Holy Spirit, but they were not yet indwelt by the Spirit.

The baptism of the Spirit consists in both convicting of sin and empowering for service. It is an error to separate these two sides of the Spirit's activity, although they should be distinguished.

~ *Saints* ~

The modern church is quite willing to hold up as heroes such men as Martin Luther King and Dietrich Bonhoeffer who were persecuted because of their social involvement — and indeed a passion for social righteousness is one of the prime fruits of a living faith. Yet the church today seems unable to appreciate martyrs and confessors like Nate Saint and Richard Wurmbrand who were persecuted because of their preaching of the gospel, which is the essence and foundation of faith.

~ *Two Types of Faith* ~

It is possible to distinguish between preparatory faith and justifying faith. The former consists in outward adherence to Christ as the Law Giver: *assensus*. The latter is heartfelt confidence in Christ as the Savior: *fiducia*.

~ Infant Baptism ~

Those who have been baptized as infants are in the sphere of the kingdom but not yet in the family of the kingdom. They are at the gateway of the kingdom but not yet in the household of the kingdom.

Being baptized as an infant does not guarantee becoming a new creature, but it does open the door to this possibility. Such a person is directed toward salvation but has yet to experience salvation.

~ New Birth ~

The hallmarks of the new birth are conviction of sin, repentance for sin, and the assurance of salvation.

~ Seeking for Salvation ~

Only those can seek salvation who are being pursued by the Holy Spirit. Only those can come to Christ who are moved and impelled by the Holy Spirit.

Unless seeking for salvation is fulfilled in repentance and faith, it will contribute to our condemnation. This is why there is not yet any eternal security for those who seek without believing.

To affirm that seeking for salvation is prior to both repentance and faith is to affirm that election comes before justification.

The pre-Christian has been awakened to the possibility of salvation but has not yet laid hold of this possibility. He is like a man drowning in a lake to whom a life preserver has been thrown. Salvation is now available to him, and yet he will be lost if he does not stretch out his arms toward the life preserver. He seeks salvation but does not yet have salvation.

For those who are chosen by God, their seeking for salvation can be viewed as the first stage of conversion. For those not numbered among the elect, their seeking is only a desperate attempt to avoid an inevitable damnation.

Those who begin to seek for salvation have a consciousness of guilt but not yet a consciousness of sin. They are aware that they have done wrong but not that they have grieved the heart of God.

Those who begin to seek for salvation have an awareness of their lost condition, but they have yet to realize that they are eternally lost apart from Christ.

~ *Two Governments* ~

It is well to note that when Jesus told the Pharisees that they should give to Caesar the things that are Caesar's and to God those things that are God's, Caesar was given only the coin that bore his likeness or image. Man, who bears the image of God, therefore belongs wholly to God.

The truth in Luther's theory of the two kingdoms is that Christians do live and work in two different spheres, the spiritual and the temporal. They are called to be both people of God and people of the world. In this twofold role they should always seek to relate the secular or humanitarian goal of justice and the spiritual ideal of agape love.

As Christians we have a dual citizenship. We belong to the kingdom of God, but we are also participants in a worldly government. It is a mistake, however, to maintain that we are members of the kingdom of the world, which is a kingdom of darkness and sin. The nation-state is under the sway of the kingdom of the world, but it is also claimed by the kingdom of God, and this is why Christians are permitted to participate in worldly government.

The Constantinian heresy signified the accommodation of the church to the kingdom of this world. We still need to recognize that there cannot be a Christian state but only a state infused by Christian values. The state itself belongs to the old aeon, but it can be made to serve and witness to the new aeon.

The Christian can support a state that acknowledges its limitations and is intent mainly on serving people rather than on controlling or possessing them. The Christian can support a state so long as it resists the temptation to become a totalitarian kingdom demanding absolute obedience.

~ *Apologetics* ~

Apologetics can silence the criticisms of pagans, but it cannot make them open to the gospel of Christ.

A certain kind of apologetics can be helpful to those who are earnestly seeking salvation but only because it holds doubt in check; it cannot induce the decision of faith or even prepare the way for it.

Apologetics is not a means to regeneration, but it can keep people from rushing headlong into damnation.

~ *Suffering of God* ~

It is possible to speak of a cross in the heart of God in that God himself suffered in the person of Jesus Christ and continues to suffer as people reject his Son.

~ *Social Involvement* ~

The kingdom is advanced not by wielding temporal power but by renouncing power, by surrendering power to God. At the same time, Christians are obliged to use power responsibly in order to check and restrain the forces of evil in society. Social action in the service of justice is surely a path that should not be ignored, but neither should it be confused with evangelism. Nor should a relatively just society be equated with the kingdom of God.

As Christians we can never identify ourselves with any political platform or program, although we may very well participate in politics. We will always be strangers in the world of politics because our citizenship is in heaven. Even if we pursue an outwardly political career, we will remain inwardly detached from the political panorama and immune to political propaganda, for we recognize that the final solution to the problems of people is spiritual, not political.

The Christian way is not to be above or outside politics. Rather Christians are free to work creatively in the political world because they are not bound to any political program or ideology.

Christians are apolitical — not in the sense of refusing to participate in politics but in the sense of not being determined by politics. They do not place themselves above politics, but they are free from the myths surrounding politics.

The Christian way is not to retreat from politics into private life, thereby disclaiming social responsibility; rather it is to participate in politics without being dominated by political propaganda. It is to recognize the ambiguity and limitations of politics and its incapacity to solve the basic dilemmas of humankind.

Christian faith is post-political rather than apolitical in that it looks beyond politics for the ultimate answers without denying the necessity for political action in the realm of the penultimate.

The Christian mandate is to set out and persevere on a spiritual pilgrimage to Mount Zion, the new Jerusalem. At times we will have to remove certain roadblocks of this world that obstruct our journey and that of our fellow-wayfarers. But the removal of temporal obstacles is only a means to a spiritual end. In like manner, seeking the correction of social evils that impede our spiritual progress must never be regarded as an end but only as a means.

The church should be concerned about both the victims of injustice and the social conditions that breed injustice.

Political action should be seen as an adjunct to the Christian mission, but not as an integral part of this mission. It may very well grow out of the Christian mission, but it is not itself this mission.

Politics can give only temporary remedies to human problems; only Christ gives the final answer.

Social involvement (in the political sense) is not itself the mission of the church, but it may be an aid to this mission.

Only those who are themselves active in the various movements for social justice in our time can legitimately protest against the identification of gospel evangelism with social action.

Robert Kennedy rightly pointed to the principal political issues of our time: peace, race, and poverty. Yet it should always be borne in mind that these are penultimate, not ultimate, issues. But can we deal with the ultimate without first giving attention to the penultimate?

The political parties today are emphasizing law and order. Should we not also speak of justice and freedom?

Faith does not come to us through social concern, but faith manifests itself in social concern.

An alliance between Christianity and right-wing politics is certainly to be condemned, but so too is an alliance between Christianity and Marxism.

The fault of the secular theologians is that their concern is only with temporal palliatives, whereas what people most desperately need are eternal remedies.

Social reform can facilitate the gospel proclamation in a negative way by removing obstacles to the faith. But it cannot make people more receptive to the gospel.

It is well to bear in mind that the church is not a political lobby but a mission enterprise.

The mission of the church includes social involvement as well as preaching, since we are called to serve God and our fellowman in the midst of the world. Yet social involvement does not mean that the church qua church should take sides in politics, although on occasion this may be necessary where moral principles are at stake.

My objection to the secular theologians is not that they call Christians to social involvement, but that they see this as the essential task of the church.

~ *Stages of Faith* ~

We can speak of three stages of faith: preparatory faith, effectual faith, and conquering faith. The Holy Spirit is active on all three levels: He inspires, baptizes, and empowers.

~ *Communism* ~

The church today must say no to Communism as well as to nuclear war. Herein lies its dilemma.

~ *Two Types of Despair* ~

A distinction should be made between the self-transcending despair of repentance and the defiant despair of unbelief. The former is a despair of oneself; the latter is a despair of God.

~ *Evangelical Spirituality* ~

The three stages in evangelical spirituality are seeking for salvation, repentance and faith, and service in love.

~ *Missions* ~

One cannot be a Christian without Christianizing. One cannot retain the fire of faith unless one seeks to kindle a flame in others.

~ *Rationality of Faith* ~

The truth of faith is not suprarational in the sense that it entirely transcends reason, but it is suprarational in that it cannot be fully grasped by reason.

~ Evangelism and Social Action ~

The relation between evangelism and social action may be illustrated by an ambulance that on the way to a hospital finds itself obstructed by a bridge in partial collapse. The bridge has to be repaired before the sick person can receive the necessary aid in the hospital. So we sometimes are compelled to repair outmoded social structures before we can help our neighbor obtain the medicine of regeneration. Yet this kind of repair work is only a means to a higher end.

~ Prevenient Grace ~

I accept a prevenient grace that is operative within those seeking for the salvation of Christ, but I deny a universal prevenient grace.

~ Disciples of Jesus ~

The disciples of Jesus were truly converted, but they were not fully converted. They had been awakened to the truth by the Holy Spirit, but they were not yet indwelt by the Holy Spirit.

The position of the disciples of Jesus is not normative, for they were with Christ but did not yet have the Holy Spirit. The Holy Spirit was *with* them, however, and it can be said that he was *in* them on occasion, but he did not abide within them as a living reality.

The disciples were in the body of Christ, but they had not yet been sealed in this body.

It is interesting to note that Jesus refers to his disciples as a "faithless and perverse generation" (Luke 9:41), since they did not have the faith to heal a demoniac. On other occasions he describes them as men of "little faith" (Luke 12:28; Matt. 8:26). His disciples believed in him, but they did not yet have a deep and abiding confidence in him.

The disciples had been converted to the way of the cross, but they had not yet been converted to the gospel of the cross. They accepted the teachings of Jesus, but they did not yet grasp the central message of the cross and resurrection.

For the most part the disciples regarded Christ as Lord and Master but not as Savior. It only dawned upon them slowly that Jesus was indeed their Savior as well, but they were not convinced of this truth until the resurrection and Pentecost.

It is significant that John tells us that the disciples of Jesus had not yet received the Spirit: "Now this he said about the Spirit, which those who believed in him were to receive; for as yet the Spirit had not been given, because Jesus was not yet glorified" (John 7:39).

For a time, the disciples accepted Jesus as the Messiah in the Jewish sense. Only after the resurrection did they believe in him as the Savior of the world.

The disciples were not only seeking, they were receiving as well. But they had not yet received the Holy Spirit in his fullness.

The disciples had "little faith" but not yet conquering faith. They had a foretaste of salvation but not the assurance of salvation.

It is not the disciples but Christ himself who is the model or pattern of Christian life. Christ was filled with the Spirit at his birth, and so it is with Christians at their new birth.

~ *Spiritual and Material* ~

The opposite of "spiritual" in the biblical sense is not "physical" but "selfish."

In the Bible, "spiritual" has a double meaning—oriented toward eternity *and* dominated by the Spirit of God. "Spiritual" can include the material while also transcending it.

"Spiritual" means centered in God, who is both holy and infinite. It therefore has a dual signification—directed toward holiness and toward eternity.

There is no absolute dualism between spiritual and physical in the Bible, but there is a distinction that must always be recognized.

We have a spiritual problem whenever injury is done to the human spirit—the dimension of our relationship with the transcendent. Since the body is the vessel of the spirit, injury to the body also harms the spirit, and therefore this too can be considered a spiritual issue.

~ *Mission of the Church* ~

In some circles the gospel is regarded as a tool for solving human problems. But in reality the gospel brings people new problems. Did not Jesus say that he had come not to bring peace but a sword (Matt. 10:34)?

~ *Children of God* ~

All people were originally children of God by creation, but God no longer counts them as his children because of sin. In order to become a child of God again, it is necessary to be adopted into his family by faith.

~ *Christian as a Convalescent* ~

The Christian is not a person who has recovered but one who is convalescing, who is not yet well but on the way to being made well.

~ *Darkness of Faith* ~

While the nonbeliever walks in the darkness of sin, the believer walks in the darkness of faith. The first clings to his reason and experience, which are blinded by sin; the second clings to the living God, who enlightens him in his darkness.

~ *Unbelief* ~

It is not inequity but unbelief that is the gravest sin of our time.

~ Spiritual and Material ~

In biblical religion the spiritual does not oppose the material but transcends it. The antithesis of the spiritual is not the material but the perversion of the spiritual—demonic and human sin.

~ The Good News ~

The good news is that one does not have to be good in order to be perfect in God's sight. We can never be good enough to merit justification by God, but we are accepted as perfect through faith in the One who is perfect—our Savior and Lord, Jesus Christ.

~ "Man for Others" ~

We should seek to be not only bona fide representatives of humanity but also people of God.

Only the God-intoxicated man can be a "man for others."

~ Creation and Redemption ~

Redemption signifies both the fulfillment and the transcendence of creation. The new humanity is not only humanity restored but also humanity elevated to fellowship with God.

The person who is reborn by the Spirit is not only authentically human but also oriented toward the divine.

~ *Holiness* ~

Holiness means not only separated *from* the evils of the world but also separated *for* a life of self-giving service in the world.

~ *Social Involvement* ~

The Christian life begins in prayer and ends in politics. Prayer is the root of Christian life; social involvement is its fruit.

~ *Natural Knowledge of God* ~

The natural knowledge that we have of God leads not to salvation but to condemnation.

~ *Barth and the Enlightenment* ~

Barth's recognition of the mystery in faith and his antipathy to natural theology point to his break with the Enlightenment.

With the Enlightenment Barth says that one should have the courage to use one's own reason, but this is a reason renewed by the Spirit of God and informed by the Word of God.

Basically, Barth has a neo-Reformation theology, but he also betrays certain affinities with the Enlightenment, particularly in his tendency toward a monism of grace, which contrasts with the moral dualism of the Reformation. Whereas the Reformers saw an antithesis between the law and the gospel, the lost and the saved, the kingdom of the world and the kingdom of God, Barth seeks to bring all of these into a higher synthesis.

~ Human Sinfulness ~

I would not say, as some Barthians do, that man is basically good. Rather man was originally good, but his heart is now corrupt.

~ Gospel Evangelism ~

Gospel evangelism calls people not simply to make decisions but to repent of sin. It appeals not to free will but to the Holy Spirit who alone can bend the human will toward Christ.

~ Law and Grace ~

One can learn that one is a transgressor by law, but one can see oneself as a sinner before God only by grace.

One must not make a dichotomy between the law of God and the grace of God. The law is a channel or means of divine grace.

I agree with Regin Prenter that only in its spiritual use does the law bring knowledge of sin. In its civil use it does not awaken people to sin; it does so only when preached in conjunction with the gospel.

Preaching the gospel without the law leads to antino-mianism; preaching the law without the gospel ends in legalism.

~ Christian Self-love ~

As Christians we must love ourselves, but not to the exclusion of others. Nor should we love ourselves most of all; only God merits absolute unconditional love. Moreover, we should love ourselves as children of God and with the power that comes from God, not as if we were gods and the whole world revolved around us. We should love ourselves with a self-transcending love that includes self but at the same time points beyond self to God and neighbor.

~ Sin in the Christian ~

The temptation of Wesleyans is to believe that they can live without sin. The temptation of Calvinists is to believe that they can do nothing but sin.

A Christian can attain a measure of perfection in faith in this life, but this must not be confused with ethical perfection.

~ Seeking for Salvation ~

Those who seek for salvation are not under damnation but under election. Yet their salvation is not yet assured, since they still have to receive the Holy Spirit.

~ Sense of Guilt ~

Just as pain informs us that something is organically wrong, so guilt reminds us of a broken relationship with God. To remove the sense of guilt would be just as dangerous as to take away the sense of pain.

~ Two Kinds of Seeking ~

The person under the sway of sin seeks for information, for knowledge, since knowledge is power. The person born of the Spirit seeks for salvation, for liberation from the craving for power.

~ Christian Education ~

The method in Christian education should be secondary to having faith. If we really believe, we will find the right method.

~ Evangelical versus Synergistic Theology ~

The Christian journey might be pictured as traveling to a destination by train. Christ guides us onto the train and even pays our way. In evangelical theology we are given a free ticket. In synergistic theology, on the other hand, we can do something for ourselves. Because we want to pay part of the cost, we argue with Christ and thereby fail even to get on the train.

~ Faith and Reason ~

Faith prevents logic from pursuing a theological problem to its ultimately harsh conclusion. The mysteries of faith are not amenable to syllogistic reasoning or straight-line inference.

The truth of revelation is in one sense suprarational in that it transcends human comprehension. But on the other hand, it is rational in the proper sense, since it can give meaning and direction to human life once it is accepted. It signifies the liberation of reason, not the abdication of reason.

~ Evangelicalism and Catholicism ~

The Evangelical stress is on fellowship, and one of its principal social forms has been the camp meeting. The Catholic emphasis is on solitude, and one of its major social expressions is the retreat house. Are not both emphases necessary in our time?

~ Two Types of Despair ~

Only despair over one's sins leads to the gospel. Despair of the world is more likely to lead to suicide.

~ Suffering of Faith ~

In faith there is a correspondence to Christ's death and humiliation but not a repetition or reenactment.

~ Sanctification and Morality ~

Sanctification is the work of God in man; morality is the work of man for God.

~ *Christian Perfection* ~

Perfect love is an act of God upon us, not a quality within us.

~ *Revivals* ~

The present charismatic revival places the accent upon the empowering of the Spirit and the extraordinary gifts of the Spirit. The next great revival will be more solidly evangelical—focusing attention upon the cross of Christ and calling for repentance of sins, both personal and national.

~ *Solitude* ~

If one lives in perpetual solitude one gains many things, but one cannot obtain character, which is realized only through the mill of personal relations.

~ *Faith and Reason* ~

We do not have the capability to apprehend Christ, but we are apprehended by Christ and permitted to see, though dimly, on the basis of his light.

~ *Bible Study* ~

In evangelical Bible study the method is not in the first instance either inductive or deductive but rather receptive—open to the guidance of the Holy Spirit.

~ Battle on Two Fronts ~

Those who would defend the evangelical faith should recognize that the battle cannot be fought on one front alone. The faith of the Reformation is under attack not only from the new liberals but also from the adherents of a rigid biblicism as well as from enthusiasts and spiritualists.

~ Sin and Salvation ~

If someone is dying of a fatal disease and a miracle drug is discovered, the only humane thing to do is to tell that person about the drug. It is flagrantly unkind to suggest that the illness has no basis in fact (as does Christian Science) or to give the ill person the wrong medicine (as do so many of the cults).

~ The Prophets and Ethics ~

It is well to note that the prophets condemned fighting fire with fire and the doctrine that the end justifies the means. Hosea reminded Israel that God did not approve of Jehu's murdering of the Baal worshippers (Hos. 1:4). In the first two chapters of Amos various nations are admonished because of atrocities against civilian populations and the practice of slavery.

~ Missions to the Jews ~

In the light of Luke 24:47 it is difficult to understand how any Christian can be opposed to missions to the Jews.

~ Church and World ~

There are some people who desire to incarnate the gospel so thoroughly that the practical effect is to bury it.

The church exists not simply for the world but for the world's conversion into the kingdom of God.

~ Folk Music ~

Because genuine folk music springs from the searchings and gropings of a free, unencumbered humanity, it can be used and baptized by the church, for it still reflects much of the goodness of creation. This cannot be said of much of contemporary rock music, which mirrors the emptiness and shallowness of a mass society.

BIBLIOGRAPHY:
THE PUBLISHED WRITINGS OF
DONALD G. BLOESCH,
1952 — 1991

Books: Author or Editor

Centers of Christian Renewal. Philadelphia: United Church
Press, 1964.

Christian Spirituality East and West. (Co-author.) Chicago:
Priory Press, 1968.

The Christian Witness in a Secular Age. Minneapolis: Augsburg,
1968.

The Reform of the Church. Grand Rapids: William B. Eerdmans,
1970.

Servants of Christ: Deaconesses in Renewal. (Editor.) Minneapolis: Bethany Fellowship, 1971.

*The Ground of Certainty: Toward an Evangelical Theology of
Revelation*. Grand Rapids: William B. Eerdmans, 1971.

The Evangelical Renaissance. Grand Rapids: William B. Eerdmans, 1973; London: Hodder & Stoughton, 1974.

Wellsprings of Renewal: Promise in Christian Communal Life.
Grand Rapids: William B. Eerdmans, 1974.

The Invaded Church. Waco: Word Books, 1975.

Light a Fire. St. Louis: Eden Publishing House, 1975.

Jesus Is Victor!: Karl Barth's Doctrine of Salvation. Nashville:
Abingdon, 1976.

The Orthodox Evangelicals. (Co-editor.) Nashville: Thomas
Nelson, 1978.

Essentials of Evangelical Theology. Vol. 1, *God, Authority and Salvation.* San Francisco: Harper & Row, 1978.

Essentials of Evangelical Theology. Vol. 2, *Life, Ministry and Hope.* San Francisco: Harper & Row, 1979.

Faith and Its Counterfeits. Downers Grove, Ill.: InterVarsity Press, 1981.

Is the Bible Sexist? Westchester, Ill.: Crossway Books, 1982.

Crumbling Foundations. Grand Rapids: Zondervan, 1984.

The Battle for the Trinity. Ann Arbor: Servant Books, 1985.

Freedom for Obedience. San Francisco: Harper & Row, 1987.

A Hermeneutics of Ultimacy: Peril or Promise? (Co-author.) Lanham, Md.: University Press of America, 1987.

The Crisis of Piety. 2d ed. Colorado Springs: Helmers & Howard, 1988. (First published, Grand Rapids: William B. Eerdmans, 1968.)

The Future of Evangelical Christianity. New York: Doubleday, 1983. Reprint, with foreword by Mark A. Noll. Colorado Springs: Helmers & Howard, 1988.

The Struggle of Prayer. San Francisco: Harper & Row, 1980. Reprint. Colorado Springs: Helmers & Howard, 1988.

Theological Notebook. Vol. 1, *1960-1964.* Colorado Springs: Helmers & Howard, 1989.

The Christian Life and Salvation. Grand Rapids: William B. Eerdmans, 1967. Reprint. Colorado Springs: Helmers & Howard, 1991.

Theological Notebook. Vol. 2, *1964-1968.* Colorado Springs: Helmers & Howard, 1991.

BOOKS: CONTRIBUTOR

"Rethinking the Church's Mission." In *Vocation and Victory: An International Symposium in Honour of Erik Wickberg,* edited by J. W. Winterhager and Arnold Brown. Basel: Brunnen, 1974.

"The Basic Issue." In *Christ Is Victor,* edited by W. Glyn Evans. Valley Forge: Judson, 1977.

"A Call to Spirituality." In *The Orthodox Evangelicals,* edited by Robert Webber and Donald Bloesch. Nashville: Thomas Nelson, 1978.

Bibliography

"Scriptural Primacy." In *Issues in Sexual Ethics*, edited by Martin Duffy. Souderton, Pa.: United Church People for Biblical Witness, 1979.

"The Challenge Facing the Churches." in *Christianity Confronts Modernity*, edited by Peter Williamson and Kevin Perrotta. Ann Arbor: Servant Books, 1981.

"Pietism." In *Beacon Dictionary of Theology*, edited by Richard S. Taylor. Kansas City, Mo.: Beacon Hill, 1983.

"Sin, Atonement, and Redemption." In *Evangelicals and Jews in an Age of Pluralism*, edited by Marc H. Tanenbaum, Marvin R. Wilson, and A. James Rudin. Grand Rapids: Baker Book House, 1984.

"Conversion." In *Evangelical Dictionary of Theology*, edited by Walter Elwell. Grand Rapids: Baker Book House, 1984.

"Descent into Hell (Hades)." In *Evangelical Dictionary of Theology*, 1984.

"Fate, Fatalism." In *Evangelical Dictionary of Theology*, 1984.

"Moral Re-Armament." In *Evangelical Dictionary of Theology*, 1984.

"Forsyth, Peter Taylor." In *Evangelical Dictionary of Theology*, 1984.

"Prayer." In *Evangelical Dictionary of Theology*, 1984.

"Sin." In *Evangelical Dictionary of Theology*, 1984.

"A Christological Hermeneutic." In *The Use of the Bible in Theology: Evangelical Options*, edited by Robert K. Johnston. Atlanta: John Knox, 1985.

"Christian Faith and Twentieth-Century Ideologies." In *Christianity in Conflict*, edited by Peter Williamson and Kevin Perrotta. Ann Arbor: Servant Books, 1986.

"Process Theology and Reformed Theology." In *Process Theology*, edited by Ronald H. Nash. Grand Rapids: Baker Book House, 1987.

"God the Civilizer." In *Christian Faith and Practice in the Modern World*, edited by Mark A. Noll and David F. Wells. Grand Rapids: William B. Eerdmans, 1988.

"No Other Gospel: 'One Lord, One Faith, One Baptism.'" In *Courage in Leadership*, edited by Kevin Perrotta and John C. Blattner. Ann Arbor: Servant Books, 1988.

"Ethics/Spiritual Life." In *The Best in Theology 4*, edited by J. I. Packer. Carol Stream, Ill.: Christianity Today, 1990.

"Evangelicalism." In *Harper's Encyclopedia of Religious Education*, edited by Iris V. Cully and Kendig Brubaker Cully. San Francisco: Harper & Row, 1990.

"A Faithful Church: Concerns of the Biblical Witness Fellowship." In *Theology and Identity: Traditions, Movements, and Polity in the United Church of Christ*, edited by Daniel L. Johnson and Charles Hambrick-Stowe. New York: Pilgrim Press, 1990.

"Niebuhr, Karl Paul Reinhold (1892-1971)." In *Dictionary of Christianity in America*, edited by Daniel G. Reid, Robert D. Linder, Bruce L. Shelley, and Harry S. Stout. Downers Grove, Ill.: InterVarsity Press, 1990.

"Expiation." In *Holman Bible Dictionary*, edited by Trent C. Butler. Nashville: Holman Bible Publishers, 1991.

"Sanctification." In *Encyclopedia of the Reformed Faith*, edited by Donald K. McKim. Louisville, Ky.: Westminster/John Knox, 1992.

ARTICLES AND BOOK REVIEWS

"Theology and Philosophy." *Quest* (Spring 1952):1-10.

"The Flight from God." *Witness* 1, no. 1 (February 1953):6-7.

"Theology and Psychotherapy." *Witness* 2, no. 1 (October 1953):7-10.

"The Bible, Plato, and the Reformers." Review of *The Rise and Fall of the Individual*, by W. P. Witcutt. *Interpretation* 13, no. 2 (April 1959):219-221.

"Creation as Event." Review of *The Doctrine of Creation*, vol. 3, part 1 of *Church Dogmatics*, by Karl Barth. *The Christian Century* 76, no. 37 (16 September 1959):1055-56.

"The Christian and the Drift Towards War." *Theology and Life* 2, no. 4 (November 1959):318-326.

Review of *Fundamentalism and the Church*, by A. Gabriel Hebert, and *"Fundamentalism" and the Word of God*, by J. I. Packer. *Religion in Life* 29, no. 1 (Winter 1959-60):154-55.

"Defender of Free Grace." Review of *Autobiography of St. Thérèse of Lisieux* and *The Hidden Face*, by Ida F. Görres. *The Christian*

Century 77, no. 11 (16 March 1960):318.

Review of *The Objective Society*, by Everett Knight. *The Presbyterian Outlook* 142, no. 13 (28 March 1960):15.

"Billy Graham: A Theological Appraisal." *Theology and Life* 3, no. 2 (May 1960):136-143.

"Biblical Religion versus Culture Religion." *Theology and Life* 3, no. 3 (August 1960):175-76.

"Nothing Ventured." Review of *Reasons for Faith*, by John H. Gerstner. *The Christian Century* 77, no. 42 (19 October 1960):1217-18.

Review of *Reasons for Faith*, by John H. Gerstner. *Theology and Life* 3, no. 4 (November 1960):331-32.

"Love Illuminated." Review of *The Four Loves*, by C. S. Lewis. *The Christian Century* 77, no. 50 (14 December 1960):1470.

Review of *The Providence of God*, by Georgia Harkness. *Interpretation* 15, no. 1 (January 1961):106-107.

"Syncretism: Its Cultural Forms and Its Influence." *Dubuque Christian American* 36, no. 2 (May 1961):2.

"World-Relatedness." Review of *Images of the Church in the New Testament*, by Paul S. Minear. *The Christian Century* 78, no. 32 (9 August 1961):958-59.

"Vain Hope for Victory." *The Pulpit* 32, no. 11 (November 1961):9-11.

Review of *The Word of God in the World Today*, by Hilda Graef. *The Presbyterian Outlook* 143, no. 45 (11 December 1961):15.

"The Christian Life in the Plan of Salvation." *Theology and Life* 5, no. 4 (November 1962):299-308.

Review of *A Kierkegaard Critique*, edited by Howard Johnson and Niels Thulstrup. *The Presbyterian Outlook* 144, no. 40 (5 November 1962):15.

"Virgin Birth Defended." Review of *The Virgin Birth*, by Thomas Boslooper. *The Christian Century* 80, no. 16 (17 April 1963):493-94.

Review of *The Restored Relationship*, by Arthur B. Crabtree. *The Pulpit* 35, no. 3 (March 1964):27-28.

"A Name for Your Church." *United Church Herald* 7, no. 10 (15 May 1964):18-19.

Review of *How the Church Can Minister to the World without*

Losing Itself, by Langdon Gilkey. *The Presbyterian Outlook* 147, no. 14 (5 April 1965):15.

"The Divine Sacrifice." *Theology and Life* 8, no. 3 (Fall 1965):192-202.

Review of *Christ's Church: Evangelical, Catholic, and Reformed,* by Bela Vassady. *Theology and Life* 8, no. 3 (Fall 1965):238-240.

"Spiritual Ecumenism." Review of *Protestantism in an Ecumenical Age,* by Otto Piper. *The Christian Century* 82, no. 47 (24 November 1965):1450-51.

"A Theology of Christian Commitment." *Theology and Life* 8, no. 4 (Winter 1966):335-44.

Review of *Ultimate Concern: Tillich in Dialogue,* edited by D. MacKenzie Brown. *Christian Advocate* 10, no. 1 (13 January 1966):20.

"Prophetic Preaching and Civil Rights." *The Pulpit* 37, no. 2 (February 1966):7-9.

Review of *Secular Salvations,* by Ernest B. Koenker. *The Presbyterian Outlook* 148, no. 7 (14 February 1966):15.

"The Confession and the Sacraments." *Monday Morning* 31, no. 6 (14 March 1966):6-8.

"The Charismatic Revival: A Theological Critique." *Religion in Life* 35, no. 3 (Summer 1966):364-80.

"The Secular Theology of Harvey Cox." *The Dubuque Seminary Journal* 1, no. 2 (Fall 1966).

Review of *On the Boundary* and *The Future of Religions,* by Paul Tillich. *Christian Advocate* (6 October 1966):19.

"The Pilgrimage of Faith." *Encounter* 28, no. 1 (Winter 1967):47-62.

"The Crisis of Piety." *The Covenant Quarterly* 25, no. 1 (February 1967):3-11.

Review of *Christ the Center,* by Dietrich Bonhoeffer. *The Presbyterian Outlook* 149, no. 11 (13 March 1967):15.

"The Constitution of Divine Revelation [A Reader's Response]." *Journal of Ecumenical Studies* 4, no. 3 (Summer 1967):550-51.

"Catholic Theology Today." Review of *Theological Investigations,* vol. 4, by Karl Rahner. *Christianity Today* 12, no. 3 (10 November 1967):38-39.

Review of *Salvation in History,* by Oscar Cullmann. *Christian*

Advocate 11, no. 25 (28 December 1967):16.

"This Immoral War." University of Dubuque pamphlet, 1968.

"What's Wrong with the Liturgical Movement?" *Christianity Today* 12, no. 7 (5 January 1968):6-7.

"An Exposé of the New Factory Farms." *The Catholic Worker* 33, no. 11 (November 1967). Republished in *NCSAW Report* (February 1968).

"Church Funds for Revolution? [An editorial]." *Christianity Today* 12, no. 15 (26 April 1968):27-28.

"The Meaning of Conversion." *Christianity Today* 12, no. 17 (24 May 1968):8-10.

Review of *The Sacraments: An Ecumenical Dilemma,* edited by Hans Küng. *Journal of Ecumenical Studies* 5, no. 2 (Spring 1968):391-92.

"Intensive Farming." *Lutheran Forum* 2, no. 7 (July 1968):4-6.

"Thielicke's Ethics: A Review Article." *The Lutheran Quarterly* 20, no. 3 (August 1968):309-13.

Review of *Glossolalia: Tongue Speaking in Biblical, Historical, and Psychological Perspective,* by Frank Stagg, E. Glenn Hinson, and Wayne Oates. *Religion in Life* 37, no. 2 (Summer 1968):308-9.

Review of *The Way to Unity After the Council,* by Augustin Cardinal Bea, and *Our Dialogue with Rome,* by George Caird. *Journal of the American Academy of Religion* 36, no. 3 (September 1968):287-89.

"The Need for Biblical Preaching." *The Reformed Journal* 19, no. 1 (January 1969):11-14.

"Fractured Theology." *The Reformed Journal* 19, no. 2 (February 1969):14-16.

Review of *Is the Last Supper Finished?: Secular Light on a Sacred Meal,* by Arthur Vogel. *The Presbyterian Outlook* 151, no. 13 (31 March 1969):15.

"Why People Are Leaving the Churches." *Religion in Life* 38, no. 1 (Spring 1969):92-101.

"Historicist Theology." Review of *Systematic Theology: A Historicist Perspective,* by Gordon Kaufman. *Christianity Today* 13, no. 20 (4 July 1969):16-17.

"Can Gospel Preaching Save the Day?" *Eternity* 20, no. 7 (July

1969):6-8, 33.

"Martyred for Christ." *Presybterian Life* 22, no. 15 (1 August 1969):34-35.

Review of *The Reality of Faith,* by H. M. Kuitert. *Encounter* 30, no. 3 (Summer 1969):272-74.

"Syncretism and Social Involvement." Review of *The Protest of a Troubled Protestant,* by Harold Brown. *Eternity* 20, no. 10 (October 1969):44.

"Evangelical Confession." *Dialog* 9, no. 1 (Winter 1970):26-34.

"Is Christianity a Comedy?" Review of *The Feast of Fools,* by Harvey Cox. *Eternity* 21, no. 4 (April 1970):59-60.

Review of *In Pursuit of Dietrich Bonhoeffer,* by William Kuhns. *Religious Education* 65, no. 3 (May-June 1970):279-80.

"A Catholic Theologian Speaks." Review of *Theological Investigations,* vol. 6, by Karl Rahner. *Christianity Today* 14, no. 20 (3 July 1970):26-28.

"True and False Ecumenism." *Christianity Today* 14, no. 21 (17 July 1970):3-5.

Review of *Power without Glory,* by Ian Henderson. *Encounter* 31, no. 3 (Summer 1970):283-84.

"Decision and Risk." Review of *Put Your Arms Around the City,* by James Angell, and *Habitation of Dragons,* by Keith Miller. *The Christian Century* 88, no. 4 (27 January 1971):133-35.

Review of *To Will and to Do,* by Jacques Ellul. *Eternity* 22, no. 4 (April 1971):50-51.

"The Meaning of Salvation." *Good News* 4, no. 4 (April-June 1971):53-57.

"Heaven's Warning to Earth's Pride." *Eternity* 22, no. 5 (May 1971):12-13, 45-47.

"Burying the Gospel." Parts 1, 2. *Christianity Today* 15, no. 25 (24 September 1971):8-11; 16, no. 1 (8 October 1971):12-14.

"'Christian' Radical?" Review of *Schweitzer: Prophet of Radical Theology,* by Jackson Lee Ice. *The Christian Century* 88, no. 44 (3 November 1971):1296.

"The Misunderstanding of Prayer." *The Christian Century* 88, no. 51 (22 December 1971):1492-94.

"The Ideological Temptation." *Listening* 7, no. 1 (Winter 1972):45-54.

"New Wind Rising." Review of *Theology of the Liberating Word*, edited by Frederick Herzog. *Christianity Today* 16, no. 9 (4 February 1972):17.

"Child Communion as a Means of Cheap Grace." *Monday Morning* 37, no. 5 (6 March 1972):3-5.

"Unrestricted Communion." *The Presbyterian Journal* 30, no. 50 (12 April 1972):12-13. (Reprint of "Child Communion" in *Monday Morning* 37, no. 5.)

"Salvation as Justice." Review of *The Message of Liberation in Our Age*, by Johannes Verkuyl. *The Christian Century* 89, no. 26 (5-12 July 1972):751-52.

"The New Evangelicalism." *Religion in Life* 41, no. 3 (Autumn 1972):327-39.

"Key 73: Pathway to Renewal?" *The Christian Century* 90, no. 1 (3 January 1973):9-11.

"Catholic Ferment." Review of *Revolution in Rome*, by David F. Wells. *The Christian Century* 90, no. 6 (7 February 1973):184-85.

"What Kind of Bread Do We Give Them?" *Eternity* 24, no. 3 (March 1973):37-49. (Expanded and revised edition of "The Meaning of Salvation" in *Good News* 4, no. 4. Republished as "Significato Di Salvezza." *Vivere In* 1, no. 4 [July-August 1973]:20-22.)

"The Missing Dimension." *Reformed Review* 26, no. 3 (Spring 1973):162-68, 179-88.

"The Wind of the Spirit." *The Reformed Journal* 23, no. 8 (October 1973):11-16.

"Ramm Reaffirms Our Great Heritage." Review of *The Evangelical Heritage*, by Bernard Ramm. *Eternity* 25, no. 1 (January 1974):36.

Review of *Concepts of Deity*, by H. P. Owen, and *The Freedom of God*, by James Daane. *The Reformed Journal* 24, no. 2 (February 1974):23.

"Rethinking Mission." Review of *Liberal Christianity at the Crossroads*, by John Cobb, and *Frontiers for the Church Today*, by Robert McAfee Brown. *The Christian Century* 91, no. 7 (20 February 1974):211-12.

"Hardness of Heart." *Cross Talk* 3, no. 3 (Fall 1974).

Review of *The Christian Tradition*, vol. 1, by Jaroslav Pelikan. *Journal of Ecumenical Studies* 10, no. 4 (Fall 1974):801-803.

"Whatever Became of Neo-Orthodoxy?" *Christianity Today* 19, no. 5 (6 December 1974):7-12.

"A New Tribalism." Review of *The Restless Heart*, by Robert Harvey. *Christianity Today* 19, no. 8 (17 January 1975):32.

"To Build Bridges." Review of *Models of the Church*, by Avery Dulles. *The Christian Century* 92, no. 4 (29 January 1975):89-91.

"What Troubles Christendom?" *His* 35, no. 5 (February 1975):18-24.

"Where the Church Touches the World." *His* 35, no. 6 (March 1975):12-14.

"New Enlightenment." Comparative review of *Atheism: The Case Against God*, by George H. Smith, and *Without Burnt Offer-
ings*, by Algernon D. Black. *The Christian Century* 92, no. 12 (2 April 1975):339.

"The Basic Issue." *Decision* 16, no. 11 (November 1975):4.

Review of *The Evangelical Faith*, by Helmut Thielicke. *Eternity* 26, no. 11 (November 1975):51-52.

"What's Behind the Manson Cult?" Review of *Our Savage God*, by R. C. Zaehner. *Christianity Today* 20, no. 5 (5 December 1975):35.

"Moltmann's Crucified God." *Communio* 2, no. 4 (Winter 1975):413-14. (First published in *Christianity Today* 19, no. 19 [20 June 1975]:28. Correction made in *Christianity Today* 19, no. 21 [18 July 1975]:23. Corrected and revised edition in *Communio* 2, no. 4.)

"Wind of the Spirit." Review of *Aspects of Pentecostal-Charismatic Origins*, by Vinson Synan, and *Jesus and the Spirit*, by James D. G. Dunn. *The Review of Books and Religion* (February 1976):11.

"A Righteous Nation." *Cross Talk* 5, no. 1, Part One (March-April-May 1976).

"Prayer and Mysticism (1): Two Types of Spirituality." *The Reformed Journal* 26, no. 3 (March 1976):23-26.

"Options in Current Theology." Review of *Thinking about God*, by John Macquarrie. *Christianity Today* 20, no. 14 (9 April 1976):39-40.

"Prayer and Mysticism (2): Divergent Views on Prayer." *The Reformed Journal* 26, no. 4 (April 1976):22-25.

"Prayer and Mysticism (3): Towards Renewed Evangelical Prayer." *The Reformed Journal* 26, no. 5 (May-June 1976):20-22.

Review of *The New Demons*, by Jacques Ellul. *Eternity* 27, no. 9 (September 1976):53-54.

Review of *The Evangelicals*, edited by David F. Wells and John D. Woodbridge. *Christian Scholar's Review* 6, no. 1 (1976):81-83.

"An Evangelical Views the New Catholicism." *Communio* 3, no. 3 (Fall 1976):215-30.

"True Spirituality." Review of *The Inward Pilgrimage*, by Bernhard Christensen. *Christianity Today* 21, no. 2 (22 October 1976):44-45.

"Biblical Piety versus Religiosity." *Religion in Life* 46, no. 4 (Winter 1977): 488-96.

Review of *Catholicism Confronts Modernity*, by Langdon Gilkey. *Eternity* 28, no. 1 (January 1977):56-58.

"Christian Humanism." Review of *On Being a Christian*, by Hans Küng. *Christianity Today* 21, no. 15 (6 May 1977):50-51.

"Defender of Evangelicalism." Review of *The Evangelical Faith*, vol. 2, by Helmut Thielicke. *The New Review of Books and Religion* 1, no. 10 (June 1977):6.

"The Mystical Side of Luther." Review of *Luther and the Mystics*, by Bengt R. Hoffman. *Christianity Today* 21, no. 20 (29 July 1977):30.

"The Pilgrimage of Karl Barth." Review of *Karl Barth: His Life from Letters and Autobiographical Texts*, by Eberhard Busch. *Christianity Today* 22, no. 2 (21 October 1977):35-36.

"Breakthrough into Freedom." *The Presbyterian Journal* 36, no. 29 (16 November 1977):7-8, 19-20.

"The Church: Catholic and Apostolic." Review of *The Church*, by G. C. Berkouwer. *Christianity Today* 22, no. 5 (9 December 1977):46-47.

"Creative Transcendence." Review of *Historical Transcendence and the Reality of God*, by Ray S. Anderson. *The Reformed*

Journal 28, no. 12 (December 1977):30.

Review of *God, Revelation and Authority*, vols. 1, 2, by Carl F. H. Henry. *Reformed Review* 31, no. 2 (Winter 1978):93-95.

"A Subversive Act." Review of *Thy Will Be Done: Praying the Our Father as Subversive Activity*, by Michael H. Crosby. *The Christian Century* 95, no. 6 (22 February 1978):195-96.

"Tensions in the Church." Review of *The Church in the Power of the Spirit*, by Jürgen Moltmann. *Christianity Today* 22, no. 14 (21 April 1978):36-39.

Review of *Final Testimonies*, by Karl Barth. *New Oxford Review* 45, no. 5 (May 1978):21-22.

"A Bleak Outlook." Review of *The Betrayal of the West*, by Jacques Ellul. *The Christian Century* 95, no. 27 (30 August-6 September 1978):801-2.

"Toward a Catholic Evangelical Understanding of the Lord's Supper." *Spirituality Today* 30, no. 3 (September 1978):236-49.

"Crisis in Biblical Authority." *Theology Today* 35, no. 4 (January 1979):455-62.

Review of *The Grammar of Faith*, by Paul Holmer. *Eternity* 30, no. 3 (March 1979):50-52.

"Donald G. Bloesch Replies [A response to Canon Francis W. Read on the Chicago Call]." *New Oxford Review* 46, no. 4 (May 1979):10-11.

"Process Theology in Reformed Perspective." *Listening* 14, no. 3 (Fall 1979):185-95. (Slightly altered version published in *The Reformed Journal* 29, no. 10 [October 1979]:19-24.)

Review of *Historical Theology: An Introduction*, by Geoffrey W. Bromiley. *Theology Today* 36, no. 3 (October 1979):452-53.

"A Catholic Examination of the Basics." Review of *Foundations of Christian Faith*, by Karl Rahner. *Christianity Today* 23, no. 25 (2 November 1979):50.

Review of *Understanding Pietism*, by Dale Brown. *TSF News and Reviews* 3, no. 2 (November 1979):11.

"Response to 'Theological Education and Liberation Theology,' by Frederick Herzog et al." *Theological Education* 16, no. 1 (Autumn 1979):16-19.

"Postmodern Orthodoxy." Review of *Agenda for Theology*, by

Thomas C. Oden. *Christianity Today* 24, no. 6 (21 March 1980):37. (Republished in *Pastoral Renewal* 5, no. 5 [November 1980]:38-39.)

"Rationalism." Review of *God, Revelation and Authority*, vols. 3, 4, by Carl F. H. Henry. *The Christian Century* 97, no. 13 (9 April 1980):414-15.

"Hartshorne, Barth, and Process Theology." Review of *Becoming and Being*, by Colin E. Gunton. *The Reformed Journal* 30, no. 5 (May 1980):31-32.

"Liturgical Sexism: A New Dispute." *Eternity* 31, no. 6 (June 1980):13.

"To Reconcile the Biblically Oriented." *The Christian Century* 97, no. 24 (16-23 July 1980):733-35.

"What Think Ye of Christ? A Test." *Christianity Today* 24, no. 15 (5 September 1980):25.

"How the Twentieth Century Is Eroding the Christian Message." Review of *The Secularist Heresy*, by Harry Blamires. *Pastoral Renewal* 5, no. 5 (November 1980):38-39.

"The Sword of the Spirit: The Meaning of Inspiration." *Reformed Review* 33, no. 2 (Winter 1980):65-72. (First published in *Themelios* 5, no. 3 [May 1980]:14-19.)

Review of *A Critical Faith*, by Gerd Theissen. *Interpretation* 35, no. 1 (January 1981):102-3.

"Soteriology in Contemporary Christian Thought." *Interpretation* 35, no. 2 (April 1981):132-44.

"Traditional Roles Defended." Review of *Man and Woman in Christ*, by Stephen Clark. *Christianity Today* 25, no. 8 (24 April 1981):56.

"What Kind of People?" *A.D. Magazine* 10, no. 5 (May 1981):18-20. (Published as two separate essays for United Church of Christ and United Presbyterian editions.)

Review of *Essentials of Wesleyan Theology*, by Paul A. Mickey. *Eternity* 32, no. 7-8 (July-August 1981):33-34.

"The Reformers Shed the Shackles of Legalism." *Christianity Today* 25, no. 18 (23 October 1981):18-20.

"A Discussion of Hans Küng's *Does God Exist?*" *Dialog* 20, no. 4 (Fall 1981):317-21.

Review of *Historical Theology: An Introduction*, by Geoffrey W. Bromiley. *Living Faith* 2, no. 3 (Fall 1981):3-5. (This is a fresh review of *Historical Theology* and does not duplicate the review published in *Theology Today* 36, no. 3.)

"Karl Barth Speaks Again on Piety and Morality, Logos and Praxis." Review of *Ethics*, by Karl Barth. *The Review of Books and Religion* 10, no. 3 (November 1981):9.

"Is Concern Over Heresy Outdated?" *Eternity* 32, no. 11 (November 1981):16-17. (Republished in *Good News* 16, no. 2 [September/October 1982]:67-70.)

"Reflections on Intercommunion." *Living Faith* 1, no. 4 (Winter 1981):13-17.

"Karl Barth and the Life of the Church." *Center Journal* 1, no. 1 (Winter 1981):65-77.

"Peril and Opportunity in the Church Today." *Center Journal* 1, no. 1 (Winter 1981):14-17. (Published concurrently in *Living Faith* 2, no. 3 [Fall 1981]:3-5. Republished in *The Presbyterian Layman* 15, no. 2 [March-April 1982]:11-12.)

"Rethinking Monotheism." Review of *The Trinity and the Kingdom*, by Jürgen Moltmann. *The Reformed Journal* 31, no. 11 (November-December 1981):29-30.

"Secular Humanism—Not the Only Enemy." *Eternity* 33, no. 1 (January 1982):22.

"Encountering Systematics as an Evangelical." *Catalyst* 2, no. 2 (February 1982):1-3.

Review of *The Fundamentalist Phenomenon*, edited by Jerry Falwell with Ed Dobson and Ed Hinson. *New Oxford Review* 49, no. 3 (April 1982):24.

"The Struggle of Prayer." *Presbyterian Communique* (Summer/Fall, 1982):24-25, 31.

Review of *Here Am I!* by Adrio König. *Spirituality Today* 35, no. 4 (Winter 1983):163-76.

"The Catholic Bishops on War and Peace." *Center Journal* 3, no. 1 (Winter 1983):163-76.

Review of *The Atoning Gospel*, by James E. Tull. *TSF Bulletin* 6, no. 2 (November-December 1982):23. (Published concurrently in *Interpretation* 37, no. 1 [January 1983]:106-7.)

Review of *The Analogical Imagination*, by David Tracy. *TSF*

Bulletin 6, no. 3 (January-February 1983):23-24.

Review of *The Faith of the Church,* by M. Eugene Osterhaven. *The Presbyterian Outlook* 165, no. 7 (14 February 1983):14.

Review of *By What Authority,* by Richard Quebedeaux. *New Oxford Review* 50, no. 4 (May 1983):31-32.

"Many Barth Letters." Review of *Karl Barth, Letters 1961-1968,* translated by Geoffrey W. Bromiley, and *Karl Barth and Rudolf Bultmann Letters, 1922-1966,* edited by Bernd Jaspert. *The Review of Books and Religion* 11, no. 8 (May 1983):9.

"But Should We Be Ordained?" Review of *Ordination: A Biblical-Historical View,* by Marjorie Warkentin. *Eternity* 34, no. 7 (July-August 1983):38.

"Apocalyptic and Last Things." Review of *The Open Heaven: A Study of Apocalyptic in Judaism and Early Christianity,* by Christopher Rowland. *The Review of Books and Religion* 12, no. 1 (September 1983):6.

"Donald Bloesch Responds [A Reply to Clark Pinnock]." *Evangelical Newsletter* 10, no. 20 (28 October 1983):3.

Review of *Models of Revelation,* by Avery Dulles. *The Christian Century* 100, no. 34 (16 November 1983):1057-58.

"Evangelical: Integral to Christian Identity? An Exchange Between Donald Bloesch and Vernard Eller." *TSF Bulletin* 7, no. 2 (November-December 1983):5-10.

Review of *After Fundamentalism: The Future of Evangelical Theology,* by Bernard Ramm. *Christianity Today* 27, no. 19 (16 December 1983):55-56.

Review of *Creation, Science, and Theology,* by W. A. Whitehouse. *Zygon* 18, no. 4 (December 1983):480-82.

Review of *Christian Spirituality,* by Wolfhart Pannenberg. *Spirituality Today* 36, no. 4 (Winter 1984):366-68.

Review of *An Introduction to Protestant Theology,* by Helmut Gollwitzer. *TSF Bulletin* 7, no. 3 (January-February 1984):32-33.

"The Integrity of the Gospel." *Pastoral Renewal* 8, no. 7 (February 1984):94, 96.

Review of *The Divine Feminine,* by Virginia Ramey Mollenkott. *Eternity* 35, no. 2 (February 1984):43-45.

"Concerns and Hopes for the United Church of Christ." *Living*

Faith 5, nos. 1, 2 (Spring-Summer 1984):41-45, 60.

"Living God or Ideological Construct?" Comparative review of *Sexism and God-Talk,* by Rosemary Ruether, and *Metaphorical Theology,* by Sallie McFague. *The Reformed Journal* 34, no. 6 (June 1984):29-31.

"Christ and Culture: Do They Connect?" *Christianity Today* 28, no. 10 (13 July 1984):54-58.

"Sanctity." *Pastoral Renewal* 9, no. 1 (July/August 1984):15-16.

"In Defense of Biblical Authority." Review of *Scripture and Truth,* edited by D. A. Carson and John D. Woodbridge. *The Reformed Journal* 34, no. 9 (September 1984):28-30.

"The Need for a Confessing Church Today." *The Reformed Journal* 34, no. 11 (November 1984):10-15.

"Cause for Rejoicing." *Pastoral Renewal* 9, no. 5 (December 1984):79-80.

"A Typology of Marriage." *The Family Album: Voices in the United Church of Christ—Theological Reflections on Family Life,* 5-8. St. Louis: Church Leadership Resources, 1985.

"Forecast '85: Theology." *Eternity* 36, no. 1 (January 1985):32.

"Sanctity." *Renewal News* 91 (July-August 1985):13.

"Everybody's Favorite Symbol." *Christianity Today* 29, no. 18 (13 December 1985):29-32.

"An Evangelical Perspective on Authority." *Prism* 1, no. 1 (Spring 1986):4-21.

"The Legacy of Karl Barth." *TSF Bulletin* 9, no. 5 (May-June 1986):6-9.

"Toward the Recovery of Our Evangelical Heritage." *Reformed Review* 39, no. 3 (Spring 1986):192-98.

"[Donald] Bloesch Replies to [Thomas] Finger." *TSF Bulletin* 10, no. 1 (September-October 1986):43.

"Be Wise as Serpents." *Eternity* 37, no. 11 (November 1986). In "Doors '87: A Special Section for Graduate and Seminary Students":D12-D15.

Review of *Ethics from a Theocentric Perspective,* vols. 1, 2, by James M. Gustafson. *TSF Bulletin* 10, no. 2 (November-December 1986):34.

Review of *Christian Theology: An Eschatological Approach,* by Thomas Finger. *TSF Bulletin* 10, no. 5 (May-June 1987):36-37.

Review of *Created in God's Image,* by Anthony Hoekema. *Interpretation* 41, no. 3 (July 1987):328-29.

Review of *The Humiliation of the Word,* by Jacques Ellul. *Theological Education* 24, no. 1 (Autumn 1987):140-43.

"No Other Gospel." *Presbyterian Communique* 11, no. 2 (January/February 1988):8-9. (Republished in *Channels* 6, no. 2 [Spring 1989]:6-8.)

"What's to Come." Review of *Knowing the Truth about Heaven and Hell,* by Harry Blamires. *Eternity* 39, no. 12 (December 1988):41-42.

"Changing People, Changing Nations." Review of *On the Tail of a Comet: The Life of Frank Buchman,* by Garth Lean. *Christianity Today* 33, no. 4 (3 March 1989):60-61.

"Reply to Randy Maddox." *Christian Scholar's Review* 18, no. 3 (March 1989):281-84.

"All Israel Will Be Saved: Supersessionism and the Biblical Witness." *Interpretation* 43, no. 2 (April 1989):130-42.

"A Reply to Paul Quackenbush [on the church and homosexuality]." *On the Way* 6, no. 2 (Autumn 1989):41-45.

"A Plan for Unity." *Christianity Today* 34, no. 3 (19 February 1990):17.

"Beyond Patriarchalism and Feminism." *Touchstone* 4, no. 1 (Summer 1990):9-11.

"The Father and the Goddess." Review of *Women and Early Christianity* and *Matriarchs, Goddesses, and Images of God,* by Susanne Heine. *Christianity Today* 34, no. 14 (8 October 1990):74-76. (Republished in *Partnership* [Winter 1991]:18-19.)

"Twenty-five Years Later." Review of *Vatican II and Its Documents: An American Reappraisal,* edited by Timothy E. O'Connell. *Perspectives* 6, no. 2 (February 1991):24.

"The Lordship of Christ in Theological History." *Southwestern Journal of Theology* 33, no. 2 (Spring 1991):26-34.

"The Finality of Christ and Religious Pluralism." *Touchstone* 4, no. 3 (Summer 1991):5-9.

"Lost in the Mystical Myths." *Christianity Today* 35, no. 9 (19 August 1991):22-24.

INDEX OF SUBJECTS

Subheadings appearing throughout the text are printed here in CAPITALS; *identical entries set in ordinary type immediately following them list additional places where the same subject can be found.*

ACTION AND CONTEMPLATION, 38
ACTIVE LIFE, 35
AGAPE AND EROS, 52, 56, 71
AGNOSTICISM, 72
alchoholism, 120
altruism, 40
anarchy, 125
ANTHROPOLOGY, 124
antinomianism, 175
anxiety, 122, 153
APOLOGETICS, 162
archaism, 7
ARENA OF SALVATION, THE, 65
ASCETICISM, 9, 129
asceticism, 21
Athens and Jerusalem (Shestov), 157
AUTHORITY, 17

BAPTISM, 26, 58
baptism: and children, 52; and
    decision of faith, 2; and Holy
    Communion, 88; and regeneration,
    58; and salvation, 16; and union
    with the church, 4; water vs. Spirit,
    58. *See also* Holy Spirit: baptism of
BAPTISMAL GRACE, 65
BAPTISM AND FAITH, 36
BAPTISM OF THE HOLY SPIRIT, 105
BAPTISM OF THE SPIRIT, 140, 158

BARTH AND THE ENLIGHTENMENT,
    173
Barthianism: and goodness of man,
    174; and Gospel-Law, 25; and
    philosophical theology, 56; and
    salvation, 6
BATTLE ON TWO FRONTS, 179
BEARING THE CROSS, 16, 92
being, divine and human, 31
BEST OF ALL WORLDS, THE, 49
Bible, Holy: authority of, 93, 117;
    authorship of, 80, 116, 130; clarity
    in, 117; distinction in, between
    spiritual and physical, 170; divine
    content of, 75-76, 144; God
    speaking in, 17; human testimony
    in, 144; inerrancy of, 63, 76, 96,
    117, 130, 131, 143, 146;
    infallibility of, 131, 143, 144, 146;
    and infallibility of the church, 157;
    inspiration of, 69; interpretation of,
    118; and matters of science and
    history, 76, 117, 131, 144; mystery
    in, 117; Reformation position on,
    93; reliability of, 117; united with
    the Spirit, 93; veracity of, 143;
    wheat and chaff in, 116-17; and the
    Word of God, 105, 116. *See also*
    Word of God
Bible reading, 17

Index of Subjects

BIBLE STUDY, 178
BIBLICAL AUTHORITY, 117, 143
BIBLICAL INERRANCY, 63, 75, 117
BIBLICAL INSPIRATION, 69, 116
BIBLICAL INTERPRETATION, 118
biblical literalism, 96
BIBLICAL PERSONALISM, 90
BIBLICAL VERSUS POPULAR RELIGION, 64
BIBLICISM, 93
biblicism: danger/perils of, 17, 111, 179; rationalistic, 70, 153; restorationist, 101
BILLY GRAHAM, 75, 104
BIRTH CONTROL, 25
BONHOEFFER, 24
born again, 90
BREAKING THE LAW, 119
Broken Lights (Görres), 43
"BROTHERHOOD OF MAN," 115

CALL TO PERFECTION, 114
Calvary: and breaking the law, 119; and love of Jesus Christ, 8; and salvation, 62, 81; separated from Pentecost, 32
Calvinism: and Law-Gospel-Law, 25; and salvation through faith, 1; and sanctification, 24; and sin, 175
camp meeting, 177
Catholicism: Anglo-, 88; ecumenical, 88; evangelical, 88. *See also* Roman Catholicism
CATHOLICISM AND PROTESTANTISM, 43, 96
CATHOLICISM AND PROTESTANT REVIVALISM, 32
Catholic-Protestant dialogue, 43
CATHOLIC RENEWAL, 147
chancel, the, 87-88
character: as aim of the Christian, 73; realized in personal relations, 178; strength of, in triumph over sinfulness, 81
charismatic revival, 105, 178
CHEAP GRACE, 152
cheap grace, 56, 70, 151
childbirth, 26
children: and baptism, 52, 65; and membership in the family of God, 83. *See also* infants
CHILDREN AND SALVATION, 83
CHILDREN OF GOD, 171

Christian academic circles, 57
CHRISTIAN AS A CONVALESCENT, 171
CHRISTIAN EDUCATION, 176
CHRISTIAN FELLOWSHIP, 68
CHRISTIAN FREEDOM, 152
Christianity: and agnosticism, 72; and alliance with Marxism, 166; and alliance with right-wing politics, 166; metaphysical element in, 89; as personalistic vs. individualistic, 132; religionless, 67; secular, 89
CHRISTIAN LIBERTY, 115
CHRISTIAN LIFE, THE, 5, 144
CHRISTIAN LOVE, 136
CHRISTIAN MISSION, 23
CHRISTIAN PERFECTION, 55, 65, 178
Christian Science, 179
CHRISTIAN SELF-LOVE, 175
CHRISTIAN TASK, THE, 150
CHRISTIAN UNITY, 68
CHURCH, THE, 75
church, the: American, 77; as the body of Christ, 132; and challenge to the world, 128; and civil rights, 42-43; as confessional, 155; and corporate reunion, 68; defined, 75; discipline, 79; and heroes, 159; as holy community, 103, 104; infallibility of, 157; and the kingdom, 85, 98-99, 180; local, organization of, 118; as manifest and hidden, 73; as manifestation of the sacred, 27; membership in, 140; mission of, 94-95, 98, 99, 116, 130, 141, 165, 166; and music, 180; and public policy, 142; renewal/reformation of, 3, 76-77; and politics, 99; and salvation, 125, 132; and sanctification of the secular, 103; secularization of, 101; and sin, 142; task of, 23, 98; ultimate loyalty and immediate concern of, 103; vision of, 60
CHURCH AND THE KINGDOM, THE, 85
Church and the Sacraments, The (Forsyth), 138
CHURCH AND WORLD, 128, 180
CHURCH DISCIPLINE, 79
CIVIL RIGHTS, 42
classical philosophy, 156
Commentary on Romans (Luther), 138

commitment: and evangelism, 129; and the new birth, 112; in a secular world, 47; theology of, 55; and the will to meaning, 54
Communion. *See* Holy Communion
COMMUNION OF SAINTS, 33, 40
COMMUNISM, 167
community of faith, 69, 80, 132
complacency, 39
Concept of Grace, The (Watson), 148
condemnation, 160, 173
CONFESSING CHURCH, 155
confidence, 147
Confirmation, 33
conflict, 23, 122
CONSCIENCE, 126
CONSCIOUSNESS OF SIN, THE, 19
CONSERVATIVE EVANGELICALISM, 96, 128
CONTEMPLATION, 153
contemplation, 35, 153
CONTRIBUTING TO SALVATION, 49
CONVERSION, 12, 41
conversion: and baptism of the Holy Spirit, 159; crisis experience of, 101; and gift of the Spirit, 33; and grace, 41; vs. life of obedience, 101; as mission, 94; need for, in Christians, 102; and piety, 88; and regeneration, 135; stages of, 161
CONVERSION IN CATHOLICISM AND PROTESTANTISM, 41
Cost of Discipleship, The (Bonhoeffer), 138
covenant community, 16
COVENANT THEOLOGY, 70
creation: acceptance of, 133; goodness of, 109, 180; reflection of, in human and demonic, 74
CREATION AND REDEMPTION, 172
creationism, 118
creative life, 35
CRISIS OF FAITH, THE, 75
CRITERION FOR ETHICS, THE, 93
cross, the: accompanied by blessing, 60; bearing of, 92; in evangelical revival, 178; in the heart of God, 163; in neoorthodoxy, 139; and repentance, 145; and salvation, 125; as shield, 16
CROSS AND THE BLESSING, THE, 38
CROSS OF CHRIST AND THE CHRISTIAN LIFE, THE, 92

cults, 35, 179
culture: demythologizing of, 45; modern, and marriage, 14; modern, and new pagan mood, 146; secular, desacralizing of, 69

damnation, 161, 163, 175
darkness: kingdom of, 79, 80, 162; powers of, 16, 94, 121; and the truth, 89; walking with God in, 7, 171
DARKNESS OF FAITH, 171
DEATH, 63, 110
death: of evil, 128; of God, 128, 152; of man, 128; and purification, 44; and salvation, 74, 83; three occurrences of, 90
DEATH OF CHRIST, 116
DECALOGUE, THE, 113
Decalogue, 93
DEFENSE OF RELIGION, 147
DEGREES OF SIN, 155
deism, 119
DEMONIC, THE, 74, 119
demonic, the, 129
DEMONOLOGY, 31, 150
demythologizers, 138. *See also* gospel: demythologizing of
DEMYTHOLOGIZING, 45
DEPENDENCE ON GOD, 8
dependence on God, 6
despair: as alternative to anguish of love, 12; and doubt, 16; in existential philosophy, 156; and hostility of others, 24; and perfection, 39; types of, 167, 177; of the world, 134
DESPAIR AND FAITH, 8
DEVIL, THE, 89, 128
devil: and demons, 31-32; kingdom of, 119; metaphorical reference to, 29; warfare with, 37
devotion: and doctrine, 109; hidden discipline of, 84; in sacred and secular, 134. *See also* evangelical devotion
devotionism, 100, 101
diabolism, 91
discipleship, 111
DISCIPLES OF JESUS, 168
DISCIPLINE, 51
discipline, 49
Disciplined Order of Christ, 56-57

DIVINE GRACE AND HUMAN LOVE, 151
DIVINE-HUMAN ENCOUNTER, THE, 85
DIVINE PUNISHMENT, 38
DIVINE SOLACE, 9
DIVORCE, 15
doctrinal indifferentism, 50
doctrinal rigidity, 50
doctrine, 88, 109, 112
DOCTRINE AND LIFE, 109
DOCTRINE OF GOD, 124, 156
DOCTRINE OF SCRIPTURE, 130
Doctrine of the Holy Spirit, The (Berkhof), 59
DOGMA AND DOCTRINE, 112
Dominicans, 89
dope addiction, 120
DOUBT, 16
doubt: and apologetics, 162-63; in Christians, 61; overcome by faith, 107
DUALISM, 79
dualism, 118

EASTERN ORTHODOXY, 79
Eastern Orthodoxy, 41
eclecticism, 88
ECUMENICAL MOVEMENT, 28
ECUMENICAL PITFALLS, 50
ECUMENISM, 90, 127
ecumenism: churchly, 90; eclectic, 88; secular, 90; spiritual, 90; theology of, 128
ego, 66
egoism, 40
election: and justification, 160; and predestination, 67; and salvation, 161, 175; of writers and writings, 69, 93
emotions, 34, 148
Enlightenment, the, 173-74
enthusiasts, 179
EQUALITY IN SIN, 8
ESCHATOLOGY, 45, 148
eschaton, 148
ETERNAL LIFE, 113
eternal security, 160
eternity, 113, 170
ethics: contextualist, 94; criterion for, 93, 94; and end vs. means, 179; situational, 109
Ethics (Bonhoeffer), 155
EVANGELICAL CATHOLICISM, 67, 88

EVANGELICAL CHRISTIANITY, 149
Evangelical Church of the Reformation, 78-79
EVANGELICAL DEVOTION, 139
evangelical devotion, 70, 100-101, 140
evangelical faith, 179
EVANGELICALISM, 56
evangelicalism: biblical personalistic vs. conservative rationalistic, 90; catholic, 125; dissolution of, in liberalism, 128; narrowing of, in fundamentalism, 128; and saints, 37; and spiritual activism, 153
EVANGELICALISM AND BIBLICISM, 153
EVANGELICALISM AND CATHOLICISM, 177
Evangelical Reformation, 88
evangelical revival, 178
EVANGELICAL REVIVALISM, 154
EVANGELICAL SPIRITUALITY, 167
evangelical theology: as anchored in Scripture, 153; and devotion, 100; and fideism, 149; and grace, 15-16, 22; and justification, 149; vs. mysticism, 113; and nature/the natural, 15, 22; as relevant to our time, 153; and the sacraments, 22, 26; and sacred vs. secular, 27; and salvation, 87; and sin, 139
EVANGELICAL VERSUS SYNERGISTIC THEOLOGY, 176
EVANGELISM, 22, 129, 134
evangelism: inter-church cooperation in, 90; in the local church, 118; and social action, 163, 165, 168; two things necessary for, 134
EVANGELISM AND SOCIAL ACTION, 168
EVIL, 44
evil: Christ as ransom to, 20; human predisposition to, 124; protection from, 86; resistance to, 44
evil spirits, 32
existentialist philosophy, 115, 156
existentialist theology, 149, 153
exorcism, 32
EXPERIENCE OF THE HOLY, 39

FAITH, 2, 16, 61
faith: activity of Holy Spirit in, 166-67; biblical, 89; concrete expression of, 36; darkness of, 171; decision of, vii, 2, 28, 67, 83, 163; in evangelical spirituality, 167;

faith: *(continued)*
evidence of, 148; in forgiveness, 82; foundations for, 155, 159; gift of, 115; in justification, 47, 98; and love, 12; made possible by baptismal grace, 65; mysteries of, 173, 176-77; mystical dimension/element of, 7, 18, 70, 89; nature of, 2; and overcoming temptation, 19; proof of, 59; in salvation, 1, 62, 65, 82, 160; in sanctification, 44, 125; and the senses, 140, 156; and signs, 106; and social concern, 165; stages of, 166; suprarational nature of, 167; and tongues, 33; transcendence of, over experience, 58; and truth, 12; and union with the church, 4; weak, vs. inactive or partial, 106, 107; and works, 141

FAITH AND EMOTION, 34
FAITH AND EXPERIENCE, 117, 140, 156
FAITH AND HOLINESS, 48
FAITH AND JUSTIFICATION, 97
FAITH AND LOVE, 11, 156
FAITH AND MYSTICISM, 118
FAITH AND PHILOSOPHY, 49, 156
FAITH AND REASON, 29, 176, 178
FAITH AND SIGNS, 106
FAITH AND SKEPTICISM, 29
FAITH AND WORKS, 141
FALLEN-AWAY CHRISTIANS, 7
FALL OF MAN, 157
FALL OF THE WEST, THE, 91
family of God, 25, 171
fanaticism, 147
fate, 124
FAVORITE HYMNS, 107, 156
FEAR, 1, 127
fear of God, 1, 33, 127
fellowship, 139, 177
FELLOWSHIPS OF RENEWAL, 51
fideism, 149
FINAL SALVATION, 42
FOLK MUSIC, 180
force, 30
FORGIVENESS, 108
forgiveness: actualization of, 108; and faith, 82; and peace of God, 41; personal knowledge of, 70; prayer for, 78; and repentance, 82; and saints, 59
freedom: and the law, 152; and law and order, 165; and the paradox of

salvation, 125; from sin, 43, 153; two types of, 108
FREE WILL, 74
free will, 174
fruits of the Spirit, 73. *See also* spiritual fruit
FUNDAMENTALISM, 146
fundamentalism: and the Bible, 131, 144, 146; contrasted with liberalism, 125, 128; distinguished from classical orthodoxy, 146; experiential piety of, 89; as narrowing of evangelicalism, 128; and pietism, 101; revivalistic, 101
FUNDAMENTALISM AND LIBERALISM, 125, 128

GENERAL PRESENCE OF GOD, 121
Gerasene demoniac, 32
ghettoism, 7
GIFT OF TONGUES, 33
GIFT OF WISDOM, 55
gifts of the Spirit, 144, 178
glory: fullness of, 55; of God, 61, 66, 70, 99, 124; as the "not yet," 28; present experience of, 55; and rebirth of the Christian, 46; resurrection to, 48
GOD, 4
God: and abandonment, 102; absence of, 54, 156; and acceptance of sinners, 111; as Creator, 115, 118; doctrine of, 124, 156-57; as Father, 115; immanence of, 119; love of, 49, 52, 55; movement of, into human history, 150; righteousness of, 46; sacrifice of, 149; speaking in Word and Spirit, 17, 64; as subject and object, 81; transcendence of, 114, 119; trinitarian nature of, 101; will of, 61, 72, 78, 80, 85, 112, 118, 123, 153. *See also* dependence on God; grace; glory: of God; image of God; presence of God
GOD AS SUBJECT, 81
"GOD IS DEAD" THEOLOGY, THE, 54
GODLINESS VERSUS WORLDLINESS, 63
goodness, 71
GOOD NEWS, THE, 172
GOOD SAMARITAN, 97
GOOD WORKS, 46
good works, 31
gospel: bearing of, on the whole of

gospel: *(continued)*
society, 130; demythologizing of, 45; dereligionizing of, 54; despiritualizing of 69; as essence of faith, 159; as foundation for biblical interpretation, 118; incarnation of, 180; as individual and social, 84; and law, 93, 174, 175; as lifeboat manned by Jesus Christ, 53-54; light of, 37; and preaching, 86, 175; precondition of, 8; primary focus of, 113; proclamation of, and human love, 151; of redemption, 68; and secular mission, 141; and social reform, 151, 166; as ultimate solution, 151; and the world, 70

Gospel and Myth, 30
Gospel and Social Reform, 142, 151
Gospel Christianity, 88
Gospel Evangelism, 174
Gospel Preaching versus Ideological Preaching, 70
Gospel Songs, 72
Grace, 30, 49, 147
grace: in conversion, 41-42; in election, 67; and law, 174; monism of, in Barth, 173-74; and nature, 15-16; prevenient, 168; receptiveness of the world to, 121; and restoration, 107; in salvation, 1, 53, 82; and spiritual bondage, 120-21; triumph of, 147. *See also* cheap grace

Grace and Free Will, 102
great commission, 68
Greeks, 49
ground of being, 4, 86, 139
group dynamics, 25
Growth in Knowledge, 126
guilt: as alternative to anguish of love, 12; and conscience, 126; consciousness of, 161; as curse of humanity, 124; as reminder of broken relationship, 176; removed by Christ, 49; of sin, 143; and spiritual exercises, 53

Hallmark of the Gospel Minister, 111
harvest, 23
healing, 153

Heaven, 85
heaven, 42, 85
Hell, 36, 102
hell: created by the cross of Christ, 37; as dimension of existence, 85; fear of, 1; salvation from, 74, 81; as taboo subject, 115
Heresy, 29, 91
heresy, 35, 162
heroic action, 19
Hidden Church, The, 73
Historical Jesus, The, 4
Holiness, 39, 149, 173
holiness: Christian vs. perfect, 55; and meaning of "spiritual," 170; scriptural, 56; and separation, 173
Holiness churches, 151
Holy, The, 86, 137
Holy, the: and the Incarnation, 138; manifestation of, 86; presence of, 36, 39, 137
Holy Communion, 150
Holy Communion: and conviction of sin, 151; dependence of, on the Word of God and Baptism, 88; transformation of the elements in, 22, 104. *See also* sacraments
Holy Spirit, 145, 148
Holy Spirit: action of, in the sacraments, 22, 26; baptism of, 1, 28, 58, 105, 106, 158, 159; and the Bible, 93, 128, 131; confrontation by, 62; and the disciples of Jesus, 168-69; emotions associated with receiving, 148-49; in enabling human love, 34, 137; and faith, 1, 166-67; filling of, 105; gift of, 32-33, 139; given to Jesus, 105, 168-70; guidance of, 178; in hearing God from within, 81; and human will, 174; as impersonal energy vs. living Subject, 32; indwelling of, 100; inner communion with, 70; praying of, in us, 77; and rebirth, 172; received through Word and sacraments, 87; and regeneration, 135; and revelation, 40, 128; and salvation, 17, 87, 160, 175; and secular movements, 147; and speaking in tongues, 62-63; and spirituality, 133; twofold blessing of, 145; withholding of, 52. *See also* fruits

Holy Spirit: *(continued)*
of the Spirit; gifts of the Spirit
homosexuality, 120, 197
HUMANIZATION, 97
HUMAN MISERY, 157
HUMAN SINFULNESS, 174
HUMILITY, 147

identification, 100
illumination, 69
image of God, 161
IMPORTANT BOOKS, 138
INCARNATE WITNESSING, 74
INCARNATION, 138
incarnation, the, 75
INCORPORATION INTO THE CHURCH, 4
INDWELLING CHRIST, THE, 105
inerrancy. *See* Bible, Holy: inerrancy
of
infallibility. *See* Bible, Holy:
infallibility of
INFALLIBILITY OF THE CHURCH, 157
INFANT BAPTISM, 160
infants: baptism of, 145; death of, 22;
their membership in the church,
104; their relationship with God,
vii, 83, 121-22. *See also* children
inferiority, 147
infidelity, 21, 26
inner life, 99
innocence, 81
INSPIRATION, 80, 93
inspiration, 69
intellectualism, 112
*Interpreting Protestantism to
Catholics* (Clyde), 61
INTROSPECTION, 25
"irreducible Gospel," 112
isolation, 9, 60

Jesuits, 89
Jesus Christ: and anxiety, 153;
ascension of, 134; atonement of,
151; and communication between
the saints, 33; death of, 20, 47, 48,
49, 79, 100, 116, 177; entrance of,
into human beings, 29, 43;
glorification of, 105; the historic, 4;
and the Holy Spirit, 105, 168-70;
humanity of, 1, 110; and
infallibility of the church, 157;
kingship of, 11; as Law Giver, 159;
lordship of, 6, 76, 95, 129, 169; love

of, 8, 92; and marriage, 8; as
Messiah, 169; as model of
Christian life, 170; and perfection,
172; relationship of, to the disciples,
168-70; as the Representative of all,
105; resurrection of, 100, 134; as
revelation of God, once for all, 40;
sacrifice of, vii, 96, 139; as Savior,
20, 43, 81, 129, 159, 169; second
coming of, 63; suffering of, 12,
163; victory of, 76; virgin birth of,
29, 109
Jesus prayer, the, 41
JESUS WALKING ON WATER, 23
Jews, the, 179
judgment, 70, 81, 109
justice: divine, 92; goal of, 162; and
law and order, 165; and social
action, 163; and war, 35. *See also*
social justice
JUSTIFICATION, 46, 91, 134, 148
justification: declaration vs.
completion of, 47; and election,
160; in evangelical piety, 139; and
faith, 98; gift of, 145; as ground of
humanization, 97; in Luther, 91;
and regeneration, 135; and
righteousness, 91; and sin, 143;
subjective apprehension vs.
objective occurrence of, 97-98;
through the free grace of God, 79;
and works, 134, 148
JUSTIFICATION AND SANCTIFICATION,
140, 143
JUSTIFICATION OF THE SINNER, 111

KERYGMA AND DIDACHE, 109
KIERKEGAARD, 60
KINGDOM OF GOD, 119, 127
kingdom of God: adoption to sonship
in, 67; as chief concern, 45; and the
church, 85, 98-99, 180; citizenship
in, 60-61, 162, 163; vs. the
kingdom of the world, 154, 161-62,
174; and marriage, 14; and
overcoming anxiety, 122;
relationship to the world, 94; vs.
relatively just society, 163; as rule
vs. reign of God, 127; as spiritual
community, 94; vs. the state, 113,
162; and union of sacred and
secular, 17; victory of, 80
kleptomania, 120

law: and ethics, 93; and freedom, 152; and gospel, 93, 174, 175; and grace, 174; and knowledge of sin, 174; works of, 46
LAW AND GOSPEL, 25
LAW AND GRACE, 174
League for Evangelical-Catholic Reunion, 68, 88, 96
legalism, 175
liberalism: and the Bible, 144; contrasted with fundamentalism, 125, 128; and the fatherhood of God, 139; and the image of God, 100; and social activism, 153. See also new liberals; Protestant liberalism
LIFE AND DOCTRINE, 112
LIFE-GOALS, 73
Like a Strong Wind Blowing, 146
LIMBO, 22
LIMITED ATONEMENT, 151
LIVING GOD, THE, 86
LOCUS OF THE HOLY, THE, 64
logic, 176
LORDSHIP OF CHRIST, THE, 76
Lord's Prayer, 78
LORD'S SUPPER, 104
love: as agape, 116, 162; anguish of, 12; commandment to, 137; as eros, 116; in evangelism, 134; and faith, 11-12; fellowship of, 69; gift of, vs. wisdom, 56; of God, self, and neighbor, distinguished, 175; human, as precondition for understanding the gospel, 151; human, transformation of, 52, 56; of people vs. principles, 71; and perfection, 55, 178; reality of, 58; in relation to law, 71; sacrificial, 66; and salvation, 62; and sanctification, 48; self-seeking vs. self-giving, 71; and the senses, 156; works of, 46, 59, 141. See also God: love of; self-love
LOVE AND FEELING, 58
LOVE AND LAW, 71
loyalty: as condition of sainthood, 19; to confessional tradition, in ecumenicity, 127; and love of neighbor, 120
Lutheranism: and child baptism, 65; and Law-Gospel, 25; and roots of evangelical devotion, 101; and two-kingdom theory, 154

"MAN COME OF AGE," 121
"MAN FOR OTHERS," 172
MARRIAGE, 8, 13, 21, 40, 45, 109
marriage: deepest tie in, 14; and fulfillment, 14; as means of grace, 45; purpose of, 40
MARRIAGE AND CELIBACY, 155
MARTYRDOM AND SAVIORHOOD, 20
materialism, 104
maturity. See spiritual maturity
MEANS OF GRACE, 59
meditation, 6
MEMBERSHIP IN THE KINGDOM, 11
mercy: of God, in biblical faith, 64; works of, 59, 77, 141
metaphysics, 89
MIRACLES, 5
mission, 94, 165. See also church, the: mission of
missionary work, 89
MISSION OF THE CHURCH, THE, 98, 116, 130, 171
MISSIONS, 167
MISSIONS TO THE JEWS, 179
MODERN DESERT, 37
modern desert, 155
modern world, 91
monastery, 111
MONEY, 80
monism, 118
moralism, 112
MORALITY, 138
morality, 66, 71, 177
Mount Zion, 164
MURDER, 64
MYSTICISM, 3, 18, 57, 89, 121
mysticism: vs. biblical faith, 89; classical, 86-87; vs. evangelical theology, 113; of existentialist theology, 149; and nothingness, 121; otherworldliness of, 149; pantheistic and monistic, 87; sacramental, 86-87; Savior, 87, 118. See also spirituality: mystical
MYSTICISM AND EVANGELICALISM, 70, 113
Mystics of the Church, The (Underhill), 58
MYTH, 29
MY THEOLOGY, 54
MY VOCATION, 3, 18, 152

NATURALISM AND SUPERNATURALISM, 138
NATURAL KNOWLEDGE OF GOD, 173
natural man/self, 74, 102
natural theology, 173-74
NATURE AND GRACE, 15, 22, 107
NEED FOR PROPHETS, 115
NEED FOR WITHDRAWAL, 93, 103
NEED TODAY, THE, 111
NEO-EVANGELICALISM, 93
neoorthodoxy, 81, 139, 173, 174
"neo-pietist," 56
neo-Reformation theology, 81, 173
new being, 42, 90, 126
NEW BIRTH, THE, 16, 46, 90, 160
new birth, 100, 106, 112, 135, 160
new humanity, 172
new liberals, 179
new nature, 16, 146
NEW REVELATIONS, 40
nihilism, 91, 155
NORM FOR CHRISTIAN LIFE, THE, 110
NORM OF LOVE, THE, 92
nothingness, 63, 121
nuclear war, 167

OASES OF SPIRITUAL LIFE, 155
OBEDIENCE, 59
obedience: and beginning of Christian faith, 156; and the biblical prophets, 86; ethical and spiritual, 59; and regeneration, 7; in salvation, 53, 87, 101, 112, 129
OBJECTIFICATION OF GOD, 115
OBJECTIVE AND SUBJECTIVE SALVATION, 44, 47
old nature, 42, 135, 146
ORGANIZATION IN THE LOCAL CHURCH, 118
ORIGINAL SIN, 107
orthodoxy, 100, 146, 149
OTHERWORLDLINESS, 149
OUR CHIEF CONCERN, 45, 61
OVERCOMING ANXIETY, 122
OVERCOMING HOSTILITY, 24
OXFORD GROUP, 24

PACIFISM, 30
paganism, 15
panentheism, 119
pantheism, 119

Paradise, 22, 44, 48, 62
PAUL AND SOCIAL ACTION, 67
peace, 9, 41, 122, 165
PEACE OF GOD, 41
Pentecost: baptism before, 159; and the disciples' understanding of Jesus, 169; and pouring out of God's Spirit, 52; sacrament of, 33; separated from Calvary, 32
PENTECOSTALISM, 57
Pentecostalism: and baptism of the Holy Spirit, 159; and demonology, 31; in Latin America, 57
PERFECTION, 42
perfection: absolute vs. relative, 114; ethical, 65-66, 75, 175; in faith, 175; and glorification, 55; in God's sight, 172; in intention vs. accomplishment, 42; in love, 178; moral, 66; new understanding of, 28; in sanctity, 24; social as well as personal, 104; and spiritual maturity, 55, 59; and standing in the sight of God, 39; way to, 21
perfectionism, 46
PERFECT LOVE, 34
perseverance, 112
PERSONAL AND SOCIAL SALVATION, 103, 132
personal decision, 16, 86. See also faith: decision of
personalism: biblical, 86-87, 90, 118, 149; philosophical, 87
PERSONALISM AND MYSTICISM, 86
PERSONHOOD, 121
personhood, 147
pharisaism, 7
Pharisees, 161
philosophical theism, 87
philosophical theology, 56
PHILOSOPHY, 30
PIETISM, 56, 112
pietism: in church history, 100; danger in, 25; evangelical catholic vs. sectarian, 68; in fundamentalism, 101; and the new birth, 112; and personal edification, 112; Reformed, 101; and regeneration, 136; and sanctification, 136
Pietists: and missionary work, 89; and possession of salvation, 101, 112; and regeneration, 145
PIETY, 66, 88, 120

piety: evangelical, 139; experiential, 89; grounded in biblical personalism, 90; and morality, 66; Protestant, post-Reformation, 145; of repentance, 89, 110; sacramental, 88, 89; and secular theology, 72; and servanthood, 71; and social relevance, 85; of surrender, 110; works of, 59

politics: and the church, 99; participation of Christians in, 6, 163-66, 173; religion confused with, 99

PORNOGRAPHY, 110

power: craving/lust for, 107, 176; and modern man, 121; responsible use of, 163; and sin, 140

PRAYER, 7, 35, 41, 57, 72, 77, 123, 153

prayer: ability of, to move the hand of God, 57; and action, 78; of adoration, 78; authentic, 6; evangelical, 72, 123; and forgiveness, 78; fruit of, in service, 77; and gift of tongues, 33, 77; in the local church, 118; mystical, 57-58; primitive, 72; in relation to life in the world, 12; as "religious" activity, 17; as root of Christian life, 173; and service, 120; in the Spirit, 77; of supplication, 57, 78; as true, vs. magic formula, 41; as wrestling with will of God, 78, 123

Prayer (Heiler), 138

PRAYER GROUPS, 12, 60

preaching: in contemporary Protestant worship, 92; in definition of the church, 75; of gospel and law, 175; ideological, 71; as pointing to God, 33; as secular, when divorced from the gospel, 86; and the Word of God, 70

PREDESTINATION, 67

predestination, 16, 67

PREPARATION FOR SALVATION, 158

presence of God: experience of, 156; general, 121; and maturity, 145; and meditation, 6; and prayer, 7, 153; as "right here," 86; and tongues movement, 36; and true peace, 122

PREVENIENT GRACE, 168

pride, 138

PRODIGAL SON, 25

prodigal son, 142

PROGRESSIVE SANCTIFICATION, 5

prophets, the, 86, 179

PROPHETS AND ETHICS, THE, 179

proselytism, 134

Protestant communities, 7

Protestantism: and contemplation, 153; and experiential subjectivism, 96; and grace, 41; and the hero, 91; and marriage, 13; presence of the Holy missing in, 36; and reformation of society, 61; and sanctification, 145; and scholars, 27; and sectarian revivalism, 32; and worship, 92

Protestant liberalism, 15, 128, 139

psychology, 82

pulpit, the, 87-88

punishment, 36, 38, 49

PURITANISM, 48, 72

Puritanism, 88

Puritans: and importance of both divine love and divine justice, 92; and sex, 48; theology of, and salvation, 158

purity, 88

---

radiance, 19

RADICALISM, 10

Radical Reformation, 14

rationalism: age of, 7; vs. biblical faith, 89, 149; biblicistic, 153; and distrust of visions, 29

RATIONALITY OF FAITH, 167

reality, 150

reason: in Barth, 173; and belief, 61; and suprarational nature of faith, 167; and revelation, 2, 141, 177

REASON AND REVELATION, 141

rebirth, 146, 172

RECONCILIATION, 23

reconciliation, 47

redemption: celebration of, in worship, 44; Christian as channel and object of, 59; necessity for personal salvation and social holiness in, 84; served by punishment/retribution, 36, 38

REFORMATION AND REVIVAL, 76

Reformation theology: and the Bible, 93; and catholic evangelicalism, 101; and evangelical faith, 179; and justification of the ungodly, 47;

Reformation theology: *(continued)*
    moral dualism in, 174; and piety of
    repentance, 110; truths neglected
    by, 79
Reformers: and demonology, 31; and
    the Holy, 86; and moral dualism,
    174
REGENERATION, 6, 70, 135, 145
regeneration: and baptism, 58; as
    crisis, 146; in evangelical
    revivalism, 6; as event and process,
    135, 146; and fallen-away
    Christians, 7; and justification,
    135; for Pietists, 145; for
    revivalists, 145; and salvation, 158;
    and sanctification, 135-36, 137; and
    social action, 168; and spiritual
    medicine, 70; and transformation,
    145
REGENERATION AND SANCTIFICATION,
    135, 137
RELATIVISM, 7
relativism, 91
religion: biblical, 64, 86, 172; culture,
    84; dimensions of, 26; popular, 64;
    and the secular, 154
religiosity, 71, 141
"religious" activities, 17
RELIGIOUS COMMUNITIES, 7, 111
RELIGIOUS EXPERIENCE, 113
religious experience, 140
RELIGIOUS LIBERTY, 4
Renaissance, 147
renewal: activism, 101, 111; of the
    church, 3, 77; pioneering
    fellowships of, 111; and
    regeneration, 135
REPENTANCE, 108
repentance: and changing one's life,
    108; as despair, 167; in evangelical
    revival, 178; in evangelical
    spirituality, 167; and forgiveness,
    82; in gospel evangelism, 174; as
    hallmark of the new birth, 160;
    need for, 102, 104, 145; and
    overcoming temptation, 19; piety
    of, 89, 110; and regeneration, 6, 7;
    and salvation, 62, 65, 160; and
    suffering, 12
rest, 150
restorationists, 111
RESURRECTION, THE, 48
resurrection: of the body, 45; and the
    disciples' understanding of Jesus,

169; as sign, 106; three dimensions
    of, 48
RESURRECTION OF JESUS, 100
RETREAT HOUSES, 23
retreat movement, 23-24, 177
REVELATION, 2, 105, 150
revelation: and the Bible, 131;
    channel of, 69, 93; in conservative
    evangelicalism, 128; and dogma,
    112; in fundamentalism, 101;
    general, 121; of God, as word and
    deed, 16; and illumination of the
    Holy Spirit, 40, 128, 150; and
    propositional statements, 105; and
    reason, 2, 141, 177; and religious
    experience, 113
REVIVALISM, 6
revivalism, 132, 145, 154-55
REVIVALS, 178
RIGHTEOUSNESS, 75
righteousness, 46, 91
rock music, 180
ROMAN AND EVANGELICAL, 87
Roman Catholicism: and baptism, 26;
    and demonology, 31; distinguished
    from Evangelical Catholicism, 88;
    and grace, 15-16, 22, 41-42; and
    the Holy, 86; and interpretation of
    Scripture, 131; and Limbo, 22; and
    marriage, 13, 14, 40; and nature/
    the natural, 15, 22, 107; piety of,
    41, 89; renewal in, 147; and the
    sacraments, 32, 96, 104; and sacred
    vs. secular, 14, 27; and saints, 27,
    37; and salvation, 6, 81, 82, 87,
    102; and service, 13; and sex, 25;
    and sin, 61; and solitude, 177
Romanism, 88
Romans, the, 49
Rosary, the, 41

sacramentalism, 32
sacramental objectivism, 96
SACRAMENTAL WORLD, 121
sacraments: and encountering God,
    86-87; and priority of the Word,
    107; and salvation, 6; as spiritual
    medicine, 70
SACRAMENTS OF INITIATION, 104
SACRED AND SECULAR, 17, 27, 69, 83,
    102
sacred and secular, 23-24, 84, 154
sacrifice, 112, 149. *See also* Jesus
    Christ: sacrifice of

SAINTHOOD, 66, 154

ST. MARY, 44

SAINTS, 3, 18, 19, 37, 59, 91, 114, 159

saints: and the Christian life, 5;
departed, 18, 33; and forgiveness,
59; hallmarks of, 37, 154; as
mountain climbers, 40; salvation of,
62; ultimate concern of, 66

SAINTS AND SCHOLARS, 27

SALVATION, 1, 6, 16, 29, 53, 62, 81,
125

salvation: activity of the Holy Spirit
in, 17, 87, 160, 175; assurance of,
101, 160; author of, 1; cause of,
82-83, 87; and the Christian life, 5,
47, 81; and the conversion
experience, 6; enactment of, vii,
125, 126; in evangelical spirituality,
167; as event, 48; and forgiveness,
108; free will in, 102, 125; as gift
of grace, 42; and good works, 129,
141; individual but not private, 45;
and infant baptism, 160; and
marriage, 21; medium of, 1; and
natural knowledge of God, 173; our
cooperation in, 82-83; as personal
and social, 84, 103, 104, 132;
possession vs. retention of, 101;
proper concern for, 40; and religious
experience, 140; in revivalism, 132;
second chance of, 148; stages of
conversion in, 160-61; and the
Word of God, 47

SALVATION AND HEALTH, 34

Salvation Army, 97, 141

SALVATION BY FAITH, 48

SALVATION, NOT SOLUTIONS, 120

SANCTIFICATION, 24, 44, 72, 124, 144

sanctification: and Calvinism, 24;
double meaning of, 144; and faith,
44, 125; gift of, 145; and
justification, 46, 145; and love, 48;
in Protestant piety, 145; and
regeneration, 146; and the secular,
103; and sin, 143

SANCTIFICATION AND MORALITY, 177

Scriptures, the. *See* Bible, Holy

SECTS AND CULTS, 35

SECULAR AND SACRED, 154

SECULARISM, 22

secularism, 130, 133, 155

secular order, 103

SECULAR THEOLOGY, 114, 141

secular theology: alternative to, 100;

and the calling of the church, 83;
fault of, 166; and humanization,
97; and human rights, 141; and
identification, 100; and new forms
of witness and service, 114; and
renewal, 77; and servanthood, 72;
and the struggle for equality, 65;
this-worldliness of, 149; and
universal love, 92

SEEKING FOR SALVATION, 160, 175

SEEKING SALVATION, 45

self, the, 63

SELF-DENIAL, 123

self-fulfillment, 14

SELFLESS SELF-LOVE, 40

self-love: and agape, vii, 116; as
Christian, 175; and misery, 157;
and quenching the Spirit, 34

self-realization, 34

self-respect, vii

self-sanctification, 44, 45

SELF-TRANSCENDENCE, 34

self-transcendence, 45, 86

self-will, 127, 129

SENSE OF GUILT, 176

SEPARATION, 56, 60

SERVANTHOOD, 71

service: Christian calling to, 63, 83,
127; as do-goodism, 141; equipping
for, 53, 159, 173; as ethical
obedience, 59; in evangelical
spirituality, 176; fellowship in, 68;
Good Samaritan, 130; in the local
church, 118; and marriage, 13; and
prayer, 35, 120; predestination to,
for all people, 67; and religious
communities, 111; in Roman
Catholicism, 13; in secular
theology, 114; vocation of, 84

SEX, 110, 127

SEX AND RELIGION, 143

SEXUAL LIFE, THE, 18

sexual life: and agape love, 127;
asceticism in, 9; and humanization,
110; myth of, 18-19; purpose of,
13, 25, 26; subordination vs. denial
of, 127; view of, in Puritans vs.
Victorians, 48, 72

SIGNIFICANT BOOKS, 157

SIN, 27, 51, 119, 140

sin: and breaking the baptismal
covenant, 21; in Calvinism, 175;
and conscience, 126; consciousness
of, 19, 174, 175; conviction of, 151,

sin: *(continued)*
152, 159, 160; as corruption, 119;
despair over, 177; and grace, 16;
and Holiness churches, 151; as
incurable disease, 44; intolerance of,
46; inveterate nature of, 49; and
justification, 143; liberation/
freedom from, 28, 43; original, 16,
107; penalties for, 61; personal and
social, 84, 178; salvation from, 74,
126; and sanctification, 143; seat of,
9; and spiritual disciplines/
exercises, 53, 61; torments of, 48;
triumph over, 81; in Wesleyanism,
175
SIN AND ANXIETY, 153
SIN AND SALVATION, 151, 179
SIN AND SICKNESS, 139
SIN AND SUFFERING, 61
SIN IN CHRISTIANS, 102
SIN IN THE CHRISTIAN, 175
SITUATION ETHICS, 109
social action: devalued in evangelical
revivalism, 6; and evangelism, 165,
168; in the local church, 118;
interchurch cooperation in, 90; in
Paul's teaching, 67; in service of
justice, 163
SOCIAL AND PERSONAL GOSPEL, 84
Social Gospel, 92
social holiness, 84
SOCIAL INVOLVEMENT, 163, 173
social justice: and the arena of
salvation, 53, 65; as concern of the
church, 164; movements for, 165;
and need for prophetic criticism, 67;
and Social Gospelers, 92
social participation, 35, 60
social reform: vs. conversion of
individuals, 12-13; and the gospel,
151, 166; in mission of the
kingdom of God, 94; and social
decadence, 51-52
social relevance, 85
SOLITARINESS AND FELLOWSHIP, 26
SOLITARY LIFE, THE, 9
SOLITUDE, 178
solitude, 177
soul, the, 45
SPEAKING IN TONGUES, 63
spirit, the, 9, 39, 170
SPIRITUAL AND MATERIAL, 110, 170,
172

SPIRITUAL AND SECULAR, 133, 141
SPIRITUAL AND THE TEMPORAL, THE,
94
SPIRITUAL BONDAGE, 120
SPIRITUAL DISCIPLINES, 156
SPIRITUAL EXERCISES, 53
spiritual fruit, 144
spiritual gifts. *See* gifts of the Spirit
spiritualism, 17, 33, 70, 104, 179
SPIRITUALITY, 132
spirituality: evangelical, 167;
mystical, 70, 139; nature and
concerns of, 132-33; social, 89
spiritual maturity, 55, 59, 65-66, 145
spiritual order, 103
STAGES OF FAITH, 166
STAINED GLASS WINDOWS, 68
state, the: and Christian social order,
12-13; and Constantinian heresy,
162; in Eastern Orthodoxy, 79-80;
as just, 13; vs. kingdom, 113,
126-27, 162; legitimate function of,
64-65, 162; and pornography, 110
STATE AS A KINGDOM, THE, 113
Stoic philosophy, 30
STRUGGLE, 11
subjectivistic experientialism, 153
subject-object relation, 3
suffering: and blessing, 60; and death,
63; and love, 58; sent by God,
purpose of, 38; for sin, 61; triumph
in vs. freedom from, 73; types of,
12. *See also* Jesus Christ: suffering
of
SUFFERING OF FAITH, THE, 12, 177
SUFFERING OF GOD, 163
suicide, 177
SUPERNATURAL CREATIONISM, 118
surrender, 110

TABOO TODAY, THE, 115
TEMPORAL PUNISHMENT, 49
temptation, 125
TEMPTATIONS, 39
theologia crucis, 39
THEOLOGICAL LANGUAGE, 52
THEOLOGICAL THEMES, 47
THEOLOGY, 126
THEOLOGY OF DEVOTION, A, 100
Theology of Jonathan Edwards
(Cherry), 157
THEOLOGY OF THE CROSS, 38
THOUGHT AND ACTION, 112

TIMIDITY, 8
TOLERANCE, 46
TONGUES MOVEMENT, 36
TRANSCENDENCE OF GOD, 114, 119
TRINITY, 101
TRUE CHURCH, THE, 78
TRUE PEACE, 122
TRUE PREACHING, 33
trust, 64, 150
truth: and faith and love, 12; and
   heresy, 91; zeal for, 134
TWO DANGERS, THE, 111
TWO GOVERNMENTS, 161
TWO KINDS OF SEEKING, 176
TWO KINGDOMS, 80, 126, 154
TWO TYPES OF DESPAIR, 167, 177
TWO TYPES OF FAITH, 159
TWO TYPES OF FREEDOM, 108
TWO TYPES OF LOVE, 116
TWO TYPES OF PIETY, 110

UNBELIEF, 114, 171
unbelief, 151
UNBELIEVERS, 60
University of Chicago, 56
University of Dubuque, 56

VAINGLORY OF LIFE, THE, 73
via dolorosa, 81
Victorians, 48
Victorianism, 72
VICTORIOUS LIFE, THE, 3, 81
VIRGIN BIRTH, 109
visions, 29, 33

WAR, 35, 64
warfare, 65, 83
WEAK FAITH, 106

Wesleyanism, 110, 175
wholeness, 39, 98
WILL OF GOD, THE, 85
WILL TO MEANING, THE, 54
WISDOM, 9
WITHDRAWAL, 41
witnessing, 17, 94
WITNESSING AND SERVICE, 18
WORD AND LIFE, 47
WORD AND SACRAMENT, 107
Word of God: as personal address,
   150; becoming flesh, 110-11, 134,
   138; and the Bible, 105, 116; as
   criterion for ethics, 94; and
   criticism of the church, 76-77; and
   the Decalogue, 113; and
   discernment, 126; and disciplined
   thinking, 51; hearing of, 17, 75;
   and human rights, 141; and
   judgment of human culture and
   religion, 86; as locus of the Holy,
   64; ministry of, 24; as movement of
   God into history, 150; preaching of,
   70, 75; priority of, over the
   sacraments, 107; and purification of
   thought and practice, 97; in
   renewal, 147; and secularism, 130;
   and unity of love and truth, 92;
   without error, 76. See also Bible,
   Holy
World of Spirits, 22, 148
WORSHIP, 35, 44, 92, 99
worship: in contemporary
   Protestantism, 92; Evangelical, 96;
   purity in, 88; as spiritual
   obedience, 59
WORSHIP AND SERVICE, 120
WORSHIP CENTER, THE, 87

INDEX OF NAMES

Adam, 25, 61
Allis, Oswald T., 5
Aquinas, Thomas, 22
Aulén, Gustav, 18

Barth, Karl: and Christian perfection, 28; and demons, 31; and the Enlightenment, 173-74; and incorporation into the church, 4; and justification, 97-98; and love, 92; and reconciliation of the world in Christ, 47; and the subject-object relation, 3; and theology of the Word of God, 55
Berkhof, Hendrikus, 59
Bonhoeffer, Dietrich: persecution of, 159; and sin, 155; and strength in Christ, 24; works of, 138, 155
Bultmann, Rudolf, 106

Calvin, John: and incorporation into the church, 4; and mediation of Christ, 78; and salvation, 16; and sanctification, 5; and timidity, 8
Cherry, Conrad, 157
Clephane, Elizabeth, 38
Clyde, Walter, 61
Cox, Harvey, 69

Elijah, 41
Eve, 25

Fénelon, François de Salignac de La Mothe, 58, 156

Ferré, Nels, 156
Fletcher, Joseph, 109
Forsyth, P. T., 85, 112, 138
Foucauld, Charles de, 58
Frankl, Victor, 34

Görres, Ida F., 43
Graham, Billy, 75, 77, 104

Heiler, Friedrich, 89, 138
Heim, Karl, 63
Heschel, Abraham, 121
Hügel, Baron Friedrich von, 19

John of the Cross, 58
Jonah, 106

Kennedy, Robert, 165
Kierkegaard, Søren: and the cross of suffering, 60; and intensity, 60; and theology of paradox, 54-55
King, Martin Luther, Jr., 159
Köberle, Adolf, 2
Kockritz, Ewald, 107

Lewis, Edwin, 31
Lucifer, 31
Luther, Martin: his Commentary on Romans, 138; and fallen-away Christians, 7; and justification, 91; and source of prayer, 78; and three types of people, 66; and two-kingdom theory, 154, 161

Index of Names

Mackay, John, 86
Mary, mother of Jesus, 44
Masterson, Father Reginald, 31
Moltmann, Jürgen, 148
Morrison, Clinton, 76

Nevin, John, 58

Paul, the apostle: and marriage, 14;
and preaching of the Word, 47; and
the sacraments, 107; and social
injustice, 67
Prenter, Regin, 174

Ramsey, Paul, 92
Rowley, Francis, 107

Saint, Nate, 159
Sangster, W. E., 51
Schleiermacher, Friedrich, 54, 120
Shestov, Lev, 153, 157

Spener, Philip, 7
Spitta, Carl Philip, 107
Stringfellow, William, 8

Tauler, John, 58
Teresa of Avila, 58
Tertullian, 30
Tillich, Paul: and demons, 31; and the
new birth, 90; and the subject-
object relation, 3
Toynbee, Arnold, 147

Underhill, Evelyn, 58
Underhill, Lee, 30

Walker, Alan, 18
Watson, Philip, 148
Wesley, John: and evangelical
obedience, 59; and sanctification, 5;
and sin, 28
Wurmbrand, Richard, 159

INDEX OF SCRIPTURES

Psalms
22:9-10 vii
27:4 61
71:6 vii
119:44-45 115
139:13-16 vii

Isaiah
49:1-5 vii

Jeremiah
1:5 vii

Hosea
1:4 179

Amos
1—2 179

Matthew
7:21-23 148
8:26 169
8:31-32 150
10:32-33 148
10:34 171
10:37 136
13:47-50 85
18:23-35 148

Mark
5:1-20 32
13:13 148

Luke
1:41-44 vii
9:41 169
10:25-37 97
12:4-5 1

12:28 169
14:26 136
16:9 80
17:21 119
24:47 179

John
book of 87
7:39 169

1 Corinthians
14:2 77

Philippians
1:9 126
1:15-18 47

Revelation
book of 17